The Ideal Made Real

or

Applied Metaphysics for Beginners

Christian D. Larson

Originally Published in 1909 by The Progress Company, Chicago

Rockville, Maryland
2007

The Ideal Made Real or Applied Metaphysics For Beginners **by Christian D. Larson** in its current format, copyright © Arc Manor 2007. This book, in whole or in part, may not be copied or reproduced in its current format by any means, electronic, mechanical or otherwise without the permission of the publisher. Originally published in 1909.

The original text has been reformatted for clarity and to fit this edition.

Arc Manor, Arc Manor Classic Reprints, Manor Classics and the Arc Manor logo are trademarks or registered trademarks of Arc Manor Publishers, Rockville, Maryland. All other trademarks are properties of their respective owners.

This book is presented as is, without any warranties (implied or otherwise) as to the accuracy of the production, text or translation. The publisher does not take responsibility for any typesetting, formatting, translation or other errors which may have occurred during the production of this book.

ISBN: 978-1-60450-006-6

Published by Arc Manor
P. O. Box 10339
Rockville, MD 20849-0339
www.ArcManor.com

Printed in the United States of America

Contents

Foreword

The purpose of this work is to present practical methods through which anyone, the beginner in particular, may realize his ideals, cause his cherished dreams to come true, and cause the visions of the soul to become tangible realities in everyday life.

The best minds now believe that the ideal can be made real; that every lofty idea can be applied in practical living, and that all that is beautiful on the heights of existence can be made permanent expressions in personal existence. And so popular is this belief becoming that it is rapidly permeating the entire thought of the world. Accordingly, the demand for instructive knowledge on this subject, that is simple as well as scientific, is becoming almost universal.

This book has been written to supply that demand. However, it does not claim to be complete; nor could any work on "The Ideal Made Real" possibly be complete, because the ideal world is limitless and the process of making real the ideal is endless. To know how to begin is the principal secret, and he who has learned this secret may go on further and further, forever and forever, until he reaches the most sublime heights that endless existence has in store.

No attempt has been made to formulate the ideas, methods and principles presented, into a definite system. In fact, the tendency to form a new system of thinking or a new philosophy of life, has been purposely avoided. Closely defined systems invariably become obstacles to advancement, and we are not concerned with new philosophies of life. Our purpose is the living of a greater and a greater life, and in such a life all philosophies must constantly change.

In preparing the following pages, the object has been to take the beginner out of the limitations of the old into the boundlessness of the new; to emphasize the fact that the possibilities that are latent in the human mind are nothing less than marvelous, and that the way to turn those possibilities to practical use is sufficiently simple for anyone to understand. But no method has been presented that will not tend to suggest new and better methods as required for further advancement. The best ideas are those that inspire new ideas, better ideas, greater ideas. The most perfect science of life is that science that gives each individual the power to create and recreate his own science as he ascends in the scale of life.

(Great souls are developed only where minds are left free to employ the best known methods according to their own understanding and insight. And it is only as the soul grows greater and greater that the ideal can be made real. It is individuality and originality that give each person the power to make his own life as he may wish it to be; but those two important factors do not flourish in definite systems. There is no progress where the soul is placed in the hands of methods; true and continuous progress can he promoted only where all ideas, all methods and all principles are placed in the hands of the soul.

We have selected the best ideas and the best methods known for making the ideal real, and through this work, will place them in your hands. We do not ask you to follow these methods; we simply ask you to use them. You will then find them all to be practical; you will find that every one will work and produce the results you desire. You will then, not only make real the ideal in your present sphere of life, but you will also develop within yourself that Greater Life, the power of which has no limit, the joy of which has no end.

The Ideal Made Real

To have ideals is not only simple but natural. It is just as natural for the mind to enter the ideal as it is to live. In fact, the ideal is an inseparable part of life; but to make the ideal real in every part of life is a problem, the solution of which appears to be anything but simple. To dream of the fair, the high, the beautiful, the perfect, the sublime, that everyone can do; but everyone has not learned how to make his dreams come true, nor realize in the practical world what he has discerned in the transcendental world. The greatest philosophers and thinkers in history, with but few exceptions, have failed to apply their lofty ideas in practical living, not because they did not wish to but because they had not discovered the scientific relationship existing between the ideal world and the real world. The greatest thinker of the past century confessed that he did not know how to use in every day life the remarkable laws and principles that he had discovered in the ideal. He knew, however, that those laws and principles could be applied; that the ideal could be made real, and he stated that he positively knew that others would discover the law of realization, and that methods would be found in the near future through which any ideal could be made real in practical life; and his prophecy has come true.

To understand the scientific relationship that exists between the real and the ideal, the mind must have both the power of interior insight and the power of scientific analysis, as well as the power of practical application; but we do not find, as a rule, the prophet and the scientist in the same mind. The man who has visions and the man who can do things do not usually dwell in the same personality; nevertheless, this is necessary. And every person can develop both the prophet and the scientist in himself. He can develop the power to see the ideal and also the power to make the ideal real. The large mind, the broad mind, the deep mind, the lofty mind, the properly developed mind can see both the outer and the inner side of things. Such a mind can see the ideal on high, and at the same time understand how to make real, tangible and practical what he has seen. The seeming gulf between the ideal and the real, between the soul's vision and the power of practical action is being bridged in thousands of minds today, and it is these minds who are gaining the power to make themselves and their own world as beautiful as the visions of the prophet; but the ideal life and the world beautiful are not for the few only. Everybody should learn how to find that path that leads from the imperfections of present conditions to the world of ideal conditions, the world of which we have all so frequently dreamed.

The problem is what beginners are to do with the beautiful thoughts and the tempting promises that are being scattered so widely at the present time. The average mind feels that the idealism of modern metaphysics has a substantial basis. He feels intuitively that it is true, and he discerns through the perceptions of his own soul that all these things that are claimed for applied metaphysics are possible. He inwardly knows that whatever the idealist declares can be done will be done, but the problem is how. The demand for simple methods is one of the greatest demands at the present time, methods that everyone can learn and that will enable any aspiring soul to begin at once to realize his ideals. Such methods, however, are easily formulated, and will be found in abundance on the following pages. These methods are based upon eternal laws; they are as simple as the multiplication table and will produce results with the same unerring precision. Any person with a reasonable amount of intelligence can apply them, and those who have an abundance of perseverance can, through these methods, make real practically all the ideals that they may have at the present time. Those who are more highly developed will find in these methods the secret through which their attainments and achievements will constantly verge on the borderland of the marvelous. In fact, when the simple law that unites the ideal and the real is understood and applied, it matters not how lofty our minds and our visions may be we can make them all come true.

To proceed, the principal obstacle must first be removed; and this obstacle is the tendency to lose faith whenever we fail to make real the ideal the very moment we expect to do so. This tendency is present to some degree in nearly every mind that is working for greater things, and it postpones the day of realization whenever it is permitted to exercise its power of retrogression. Many a person has fallen into chronic despondency after having had a glimpse of the ideal, because it was so very beautiful, so very desirable, in fact, the only one thing that could satisfy, and yet seemingly so far away and so impossible to reach. But here is a place where we must exercise extraordinary faith. We must never recognize the gulf that seems to exist between our present state and the state we desire to reach. On the other hand, we must continue in the conviction that the gulf is only seeming and that we positively shall reach the ideal that appears in the splendors of what seems to be a distant future, although what actually is very near at hand.

Those who have more faith and more determination do not, as a rule, fall down when they meet this seeming gulf; they inwardly know that every ideal will some time be realized. It could not be otherwise, because what we see in the distance is invariably something that lies in the pathway of our own eternal progress, and if we continue to move forward we must inevitably reach it. But even to these the ideal does at times appear to be very far away, and the time of waiting seems very long. They are frequently on the verge of giving up and fears arise at intervals that many unpleasant experiences may, after all, be met before the great day of realization is gained; however, we cannot afford to entertain such fears for a moment nor to think that anything unpleasant can transpire during the period of transition; that is, the passing from the imperfections of present conditions to the joys and delights of an ideal life. We must remember that fear and despondency invariably retard our progress, no matter what our object in view may be, and that discouragement is very liable to cause a break in the engine that is to take our train to the fair city we so long have desired to reach.

The time of waiting may seem long during such moments as come when the mind is down, but so long as the mind is on the heights the waiting time disappears, and the pleasure of pursuit comes to take its place. In this connection we should remember that the more frequently we permit the mind to fall down into fears and doubts the longer we shall have to wait for the realization of the ideal; and the more we live in the upper story of life the sooner we shall reach the goal in view. There are many who give up temporarily all efforts toward reaching their ideals, thinking it is impossible and that nothing is gained by trying, but such minds should realize that they are simply making their future progress more difficult by retarding their present progress. Such minds should realize the great fact that every ideal can be made real, because nothing is impossible.

To reach any desired goal the doing of certain things is necessary, but if those things are not done now they will have to be done later; besides, when we give up in the present we always make the obstacles in our way much greater than they were before. Those things that are necessary to promote our progress become more difficult to do the longer we remain in what may be termed the "giving up" attitude, and the reason why is found in the fact that the mind that gives up becomes smaller and smaller; it loses ability, capacity and power and becomes less and less competent to cope with the problems at hand. Whenever we give up we invariably fall down into a smaller mental state. When we cease to move forwards we begin to move backwards. We retard progression only when we cease to promote progression. On the other hand, so long as we continue to pursue the ideal we ascend into larger and larger mental states, and thus increase our power to make real the ideals that are before us. The belief that it is impossible to make real the ideal has no foundation whatever in truth. It is simply an illusion produced by fear and has no place in the exact science of life. When you discern an ideal you discover something that lies in your own onward path. Move forward and you simply cannot fail to reach it; but when you are to reach the coveted goal depends upon how rapidly you are moving now. Knowing this, and knowing that fear, doubt, discouragement and indifference invariably retard this forward movement, we shall find it most profitable to remove those mental states absolutely.

The true attitude is the attitude of positive conviction; that is, to live in the strong conviction that whatever we see before us in the ideal will positively be realized, sooner or later, if we only move forward, and we can make it sooner if we will move forward steadily, surely and rapidly during every moment of the great eternal now. To move forward steadily during the great eternal now is to realize now as much of the ideal as we care to appropriate now; no waiting therefore is necessary. To begin to move forward is to begin to make real the ideal, and we will realize in the now as much of the ideal as is necessary to make the now full and complete. To move forward steadily during the great eternal now is to eternally become more than you are; and to become more than you are is to make yourself more and more like your ideal; and here is the great secret, because the principle is that you will realize your ideal when you become exactly like your ideal, and that you will realize as much of your ideal now as you develop in yourself now. The majority, however, feel that they can never become as perfect as their ideal; others, however, think that they can, and that they will sometime, but that it will require ages, and they dwell constantly upon the unpleasant belief that they may in the meantime have to pass through years and years of ordinary and undesirable experience; but they are mistaken, and besides, are retarding their own progress every moment by entertaining such thoughts.

If all the time and all the energy that is wasted in longing and longing, yearning and yearning were employed in scientific, practical self development, the average person would in a short time become as perfect as his ideal. He would thus realize his ideal, because we attract from the without what corresponds exactly to what is active in our own within. When we attain the ideal and the beautiful in our own natures, we shall meet the ideal and the beautiful wherever we may go in the world, and we will find the same things in the real that we dreamed of in the ideal. When we see an ideal we usually begin to long for it and hope that something remarkable may happen so as to bring it into our possession, and we thus continue to long and yearn and wait with periods of despondency intervening. We simply use up time and energy to no avail. When we see an ideal the proper course to pursue is to begin at once to develop that ideal in our own nature. We should never stop to wait and see whether it is coming true or not, and we should never stop to figure how much time it may require to reach our goal. The secret is, begin now to be like your ideals, and at the proper time that ideal will be made real.

The very moment you begin to rebuild yourself in the exact likeness of your ideal you will begin to realize your ideal, because we invariably gain possession of that of which we become conscious; and to begin to develop the ideal in ourselves is to begin to become conscious of the ideal. To give thought to time is to stop and measure time in consciousness, and every stop in consciousness means retarded progress. Real progress is eternal; it is a forward movement that is continuous now, and in the realization of such a progress no thought is ever given to time. To live in the life of eternal progress is to gain ground every moment. It means the perpetual increase of everything that has value, greatness and worth, and the mind that lives in such a life cannot possibly be discouraged or dissatisfied. Such a mind will not only live in the perpetual increase of everything that heart can wish for, but will also realize perpetually the greatest joy of all joys, the joy of going on. The discouraged mind is the mind that lives in the emptiness of life, but there can be no emptiness in that life that lives in the perpetual increase of all that is good and beautiful and ideal.

The only time that seems long is the time that is not well employed in continuous attainment, and the only waiting time, that seems the hardest time of all, is the time that is not fully consecrated to the highest purpose you have in view. When we understand that we all may have different ideals we will find that we have an undeveloped correspondent in ourselves to every ideal that we may discern, and if we proceed to develop these corresponding parts there will be some ideals realized every day. Today we may succeed in making real an ideal that we first discovered a year ago. Tomorrow we may reach a goal towards which we have been moving for years, and in a few days we may realize ideals that we have had in view during periods of time varying from a few weeks to several years; and if we are applying the principles that underlie the process of making real the ideal, we may at any time realize ideals of which we have dreamed for a life time. Consequently, when we approach this subject properly we shall daily come into the possession of something that is our own. All the beautiful things of which we have dreamed will be coming into our world and there will be new arrivals every day.

This is the life of the real idealist, and we cannot picture a life that is more complete and more satisfying; but it is not only complete in the present. It is constantly growing larger and more desirable, thus giving us daily a higher degree of satisfaction and joy. When we discern an ideal that ideal has come within the circle of our own capacity for development, and the power to develop that ideal in ourselves is therefore at hand. The mind never discerns those ideals that are beyond the possibility of present development. Thus we realize that when an ideal is discerned it is proof positive that we have the power to make it real now.

Those who have not found their ideals in any shape or form whatever have simply neglected to make their own ideal nature strong, positive and pronounced. To live in negative idealism is to continue to dream on without seeing a single dream come true; but when the ideals we discern in our own natures become strong, positive working forces our dreams will soon come true; our ideals will be realized one after the other until life becomes what it is intended to be, a perpetual ascension into all that is rich, beautiful and sublime.

Whether we speak of environments, attainments, achievements, possessions, circumstances, opportunities, friends, companions or the scores of things that belong in our world, the law is the same. We receive an ideal only when we become just like that ideal. If we seek better friends, we shall surely find them and retain them, if we develop higher and higher degrees of friendship. If we wish to associate with refined people, we must become more refined in action, thought and speech. If we wish to reach our ideals in the world of achievement, we must develop greater ability, capacity and power. If we desire better environments, we must not only learn to appreciate the beautiful, but must also develop the power to produce those things that have true \quality, high worth and real superiority. The great secret is to become more useful in the world; that is, useful in the largest and highest sense of that term. He who gives his best to the world will receive the best in return.

The world needs able men and women; people who can do things that are thoroughly worth while; people who can think great thoughts and transform such thoughts into great deeds; and to secure such men and women the world will give anything that it may hold in its possession. To make real the ideal, proceed to develop greatness, superiority and high worth in yourself. Train the mind to dwell constantly upon the borderland of the highest ideals that you can possibly picture; but do not simply yearn for what you can see, and do not covet what has not yet become your own. Proceed to remake yourself into the likeness of that ideal and it will become your own. To proceed with this great development, the whole of life must be changed to conform with the exact science of life; that is, that science that is based upon the physical and the metaphysical united as the one expression of all that is great and sublime in the soul. The new way of thinking about things, viewing things and doing things must be adopted in full, and this new way is based upon the principle that the ideal actually is real, and therefore should be approached not as a future possibility, but as a present actuality. Think of the ideal as if it were real and you will find it to be real. Meet all things as if they contained the ideal, and you will find that all things will present their ideals to you, not simply as mere pictures, but as realities. View the whole of life from the heights of existence; then you will see things as they are and deal with things accordingly; you will see that side of the whole of existence that may be termed the better side, and in consequence, you will grow into the likeness of that better side. When you grow into the likeness of the better side of all things, you will attract the better side of all things, and the ideal in everything in the world will be made real in your world.

How To Begin: The Prime Essentials

To formulate rules in detail that will apply to each individual case is neither possible nor necessary. All have not the same present needs nor the same previous training; but there are certain general principles that apply to all, and these, if followed according to the individual viewpoint, will produce the results desired. If the proper beginning is made, the subsequent results will not only be greater and be realized in less time, but much useless experience and delay will be avoided. These principles, or prime essentials, are as follows:

1. Learn to be still. When you undertake to live an ideal life and seek to promote your advancement in every direction, you will find that much cannot be gained until your entire being is placed in a proper condition for growth; the reason being that the ideal is ever advancing toward higher ideals, and you must improve yourself before you can better your life. It has been found that all laws of growth require order, harmony and stillness for proper action; therefore, to live peacefully, think peacefully, act peacefully and speak peacefully are important essentials. This will not only put the entire being into proper condition for growth, but will also conserve energy, and when you begin to live the larger life you will want to use properly all your forces; neither misusing or wasting anything. To acquire stillness never "try hard," but simply exercise general self control in everything you do. Never be anxious about results, and they will come with less effort, and in less time. Whenever you have a moment to spare relax the whole person, mind and body; just let everything fall into the easiest position possible. Make no effort to relax, simply let go. So long as you try to relax you will not succeed.

While in this relaxed condition be quiet; do not move a muscle; breathe deeply but gently, and think only of peace and stillness. Before you go to sleep at night relax your entire system, and fall asleep with peace in your mind; bathe your mind and body, so to speak, in the crystal sea of the beautiful calm. These methods alone will work wonders in a few weeks. While you are at work hold yourself from anxious hurry or disturbed action; work in the attitude of poise and you will accomplish much more in the same given time and you will be a far better workman. Train yourself to come into the realization of perfect peace by gently holding a deep strong desire for peace and by ordering all your actions to harmonize with the peaceful goal in view. The result will be "the peace that passeth understanding," and for this alone your gratitude will be both boundless and endless.

2. Rejoice and be glad. Cheerfulness is not only a good medicine, but it is food for mind and body. The cheerful life will fill every atom with new life, and it is to the faculties of the mind what sunshine is to the flowers and trees. To be happy always is one of the greatest things that man can do, and there are few things that are more profitable in every sense of that term. No matter what comes, be glad; and live in the conviction that all things are working together for good to you. As your conviction is so is your faith; and as your faith is so it shall be unto you. When you live in the conviction that all things are working together for good you will cause all things to work together for good, and you will understand the reason why when you begin to apply the real science of ideal living. No matter how dark the cloud, look for the silver lining; it is there, and when you always look at the bright side of things you develop brightness in yourself. This brightness will strengthen all your faculties so that you can easily overcome what obstacles may be in your way, and thus gain the victory desired. Direct your attention constantly to the bright side of things; refuse absolutely to consider any other side. At first this may not be possible in the absolute sense, but perseverance never fails to win. However, do not try hard; gently direct your attention to the bright side and know that you can. Ere long it will be second nature for you to live on the sunny side. The value of this attainment is very great; first, because joyousness will increase life, power, energy and force; this we all know from personal experience, and we wish to have all the life and power that we can possibly secure; second, because the happiest soul never worries, which is great gain. Worry has crippled thousands of fine minds and brought millions to an early grave. We simply cannot afford to worry and must never do so under any condition

whatever. If we have that habit we can remove it at once by the proper antidote, which is joyousness. After you have trained yourself to look only for the bright and the best, the bright and the best will come to you, because you will be using your powers to bring those very things to pass; therefore, rejoice and be glad every moment. Let your heart and your soul sing at all times. When you do not feel the joyous music within, produce it with your own imagination, and ere long it will come of itself with greater and greater abundance; your soul will want to sing because it feels music, and there are few joys that equal the joy that comes when music is felt in the soul. There are so many things that are sweet and beautiful in life that when we once find the key to harmony we shall always rejoice. In the meantime, be happy for the good you have found, and through that very attitude you will develop the power to attract better things than you ever had before. This personal existence is brimful of good things and happy souls will find them all.

3. Love everybody and be kind. If you wish your path to be strewn with roses, just be kind. Give your best to the world, and the best will come to you without fail; if it does not come today, never mind; just go on being kind and refuse to consider disappointments. Never hold in mind those things that you do not wish to retain; you thus cause those things to pass away. This "shall also pass away" is true of everything that is not pleasant; but unpleasant things will not pass away so long as we hold them in thought. That which you let go from your mind will pass away from you entirely. Train yourself to be kindness in a permanent state of mind, because you cannot afford to criticize, condemn or be angry at any time. We know that anger not only disturbs the mind, but also destroys the cells of the body, and no one can be angry without losing a great deal of life and energy. To find fault never pays; it simply brings enmity, discord and criticisms; besides, the faults we constantly see in others will develop in ourselves. The critical mind is destructive and the critical attitude is weakening to the entire system; therefore, no one can be his best who permits himself to think or talk about the flaws of life. Be good and kind to everybody; it is one of the royal paths to happiness and peace. When anyone does wrong, do not condemn; help him out; help him find the better way. "Cast your bread upon the waters;" it will surely return; sometimes more quickly than you expect it. Therefore, give abundantly of all that is best in your life, and nothing is better than kindness and love. When you begin to live an ideal life you will desire more and more to live the largest life possible, and to accomplish this you must learn to be much to everybody. Your purpose must

be to be useful in the largest and truest sense of that term; and nothing can promote this purpose so thoroughly and so extensively as universal kindness. This does not imply, however, that you are to permit yourself to be imposed upon or unjustly used by the unscrupulous. It is our duty, as well as our privilege to demand the right at all times, and to demand justice for everybody and from everybody, but this should be done in kindness, with the antagonistic attitude eliminated. The love that loves everybody is not the love that seeks to gain personal possession of some object of affection. We refer to that larger kindness that excludes no one from our whole souled good wishes. This form of love is the greatest power in the world, and the one who loves the most in this larger, truer sense will accomplish the most. The reason why is found in the fact that a great love invariably brings out all that is large, great and extraordinary in human nature. To state that the one who takes the greatest interest in the welfare of the world does the most to promote his own interests may seem to be a contradiction of terms; but it is true, and it proves conclusively that the one who gives his best to the world will invariably receive the best in return. Never permit yourself to say that you cannot love every creature that lives; say that you do love everything that lives, and mean it. What you say you are doing that you will find yourself doing. This greater love illumines the mind, gives new life to every fibre in your being, removes almost every burden and eases the whole path of existence. Love removes entirely all anger, hatred, revenge, ill will, and similar states, a matter of great importance, for no one can live an ideal life while such states of mind remain. To have a sweet temper and loving disposition and a kind heart is worth more than tons of gold. We are all finding this to be true, and we realize fully that the person who loves everybody with that larger loving kindness has taken a long step upward into that life that is real life. This is not mere sentiment, but the expression of an exact scientific fact. A strong, continuous love will bring all good to any one who lives and acts as he inwardly feels.

4. Have faith in abundance. Have faith in God; have faith in man; have faith in yourself; have faith in faith. Believe in everything, and you relate yourself to the best that is in everything. We all know the value of self confidence, but faith is infinitely deeper, larger and higher. Self confidence helps us to believe in ourselves, as we are at present, and thus helps us to make a better use of the talents we now possess; but faith elevates the mind into the consciousness of our larger and superior possibilities, and thus increases perpetually the power, the capacity and

the efficiency of the talents we now possess. Faith brings out the best that is within us and puts that best to work now. He who follows faith may frequently go out upon the seeming void, but he always finds the solid rock, The reason is that faith has superior vision and goes instinctively to the very thing we desire to find. Faith does not expect things to come of themselves. Faith never stands and waits; it does things; but while at work believes that the goal will be reached and the undertaking accomplished. The person who works in the attitude of faith can never fail; because through faith he draws upon the inexhaustible. The person who works in the attitude of doubt can never be at his best. Through the feeling of doubt he lowers his own ability; he holds back his best power and employs but a portion of his capacity; but the one who works in faith will press on to the very limit of his present capacity and then go on further still, because the more faith he has the more fully he realizes that there is no limit to his capacity, that the seeming void that lies before is positively solid rock all the way and he may safely proceed. Whatever you do believe that you can succeed in; do not for a moment permit yourself to doubt; know that the Infinite is your source, that you live in the universal and have the boundless upon which to draw for supply. If people or things do not come up to your ideal never mind; give them time; continue to have faith in their better selves; they will also scale the heights. Expect them all to do their best, and most of them will do so now; the others will soon follow, if you live in the faith that they will. The unbounded faith of one soul can elevate the lives of thousands. This is a statement that is just as true as it is great, and we should constantly give it the highest place in mind. The man who has faith in the whole race is an inspiration to everybody. Many a person has risen rapidly in the scale because some one had faith in him. Faith is the greatest elevating power that we know in the world. Faith can convert any failure into success and can promote the advancement of everybody, no matter what the circumstances may be. Have faith in yourself and you will advance as you never advanced before. Have faith in others and they will inevitably follow. Have faith in the Infinite and the Supreme Power will always be with you. This power will see you through, whatever your goal may be. Therefore, if you would enter the new life, the better life, the ideal life, and inspire others to do the same, have faith in abundance.

5. Pray without ceasing. The true prayer is the whole souled desire for the larger, the higher and the better while the mind is stayed upon the Most High; and to pray without ceasing is to constantly live in that lofty

desire. The forces of mind and body always follow our desires; therefore, if we would use our powers in building up a larger life we must have high desires and true desires. Turn your desires upward and keep them there; desire the greater things only; never desire anything less. Those powers within you will cause you to become as true, as great and as perfect as your heart has prayed that you might become. To cause our desires, thoughts and states of consciousness to rise to the very highest states of being, we should employ the silence daily; that is, we should enter into the absolute stillness of the secret life of the soul. Through the silence we shall find the secret of secrets, the path to that inner world from which everything proceeds. To begin, be alone and comfortably seated. Or, you may enter the silence in association with someone that is in perfect harmony with yourself. Relax mind and body; close your eyes and be perfectly quiet; turn your attention upon the inner life of the soul and gently hold your mind upon the thoughts of stillness and peace. Affirm with deep, quiet feeling, "Peace is mine." "I am resting in the stillness of the spirit." "I have entered the beautiful calm." "I am one with the Infinite." "I am in the kingdom of the great within." "I am in the secret places of the Most High," and similar states. While you make these statements feel that you are peaceful and still and that you are now in that inner world where all is quiet and serene. When you feel this deep, sublime stillness you can use other affirmations according to your present needs. You may affirm that you are well and strong and happy and harmonious, and that you have full possession of all those qualities that you know have existence in real life. To feel the perfect peace of the soul, however, is the first essential. After that is attained your consciousness will deepen and you will enter the great within to a greater and greater degree. While the mind is in this interior state of being every thought you think will be a power, and every desire you express will modify or change everything in your life according to the nature of that desire and in proportion to its depth and unity with the Supreme. For this reason you should train yourself to think only right thoughts and create only the truest desires while you are in the silent state. That which you think or do while in the silence will have a greater effect upon your life than that which you may attempt while on the surface of outer consciousness. Therefore, everything that is important should be taken into the silence and through the silence to the Infinite. This corresponds perfectly with the statement "Take it to the Lord in prayer." The real purpose of the silence is to enable the mind to enter the inner life and not only recreate all thought according to the higher truth, but to enter into a more perfect touch with the divine source of things. The silence should be entered every day for ten, twenty or thirty minutes. This is a daily practice of extreme value. Though you may not have any real results at first, simply continue; you will reach your goal. When you begin to become conscious of your interior life and begin to live more or less in touch with the world beautiful that is within you, you will find that you can live in this high, peaceful state the greater part of the time and thus be in the silence almost constantly. This is not only a most desirable attainment, but it is the one great attainment toward which every soul should work. When a person can live in these higher realms always and constantly, and desire the realization of the highest and the best that he knows, the prayer without ceasing, the true spiritual prayer is being fulfilled. Such a prayer will be answered eternally. Every day will bring us something that we truly wished for, and every moment will be supplied with all that is necessary to make the present full and complete.

6. Think the truth. When we learn to think the truth we have actually come to the "parting of the ways." Here we find where the old leaves off and the new begins. In this state the wrong disappears and the right is discerned and realized in an ever increasing manner. The foundation of all truth is expressed in the basic statement "Man is a Spiritual Being Created in the Image And Likeness Of God". Being created in the image of God man is now divine and in possession of all the divine attributes. Each individual is now in possession of infinite wisdom, infinite power, infinite love, eternal life, perfect peace, everlasting joy, universal truth, universal freedom, universal good, divine wholeness, spotless virtue, boundless supply. True, these attributes exist principally in the potential state, that is, they are possibilities waiting in the within for unfoldment, development and expression; nevertheless, they do exist in every soul and to a degree that is limitless. Therefore, every soul does actually possess those attributes, and to speak the truth we must recognize their existence and even now claim their possession. To think the truth you must think that you are divine in your true being, and that you possess these attributes, because this is the truth. You are divine in your true being, because you are created in the image of God, and you do possess the divine attributes just mentioned because that which is divine must necessarily possess the attributes of the divine. To think contrary to this would be wrong thought, and from wrong thought comes all the wrong in the world. The average person does think contrary to this

thought; therefore, he is almost constantly in bondage to sin, sickness or trouble of some kind. Divine wholeness, that is, perfect health of body and mind is yours now, always was and always will be; therefore it would be wrong for you to say, "I am sick." Your real being is never sick, never will be, because it is divine and you are the real being; you are not the body; you possess a body, and that body may be indisposed, if you create wrong thought, but that body is not you. You are a spiritual being created in the image of God, therefore you are always well. When sickness appears on the surface, that is, in the body, know that it is on the surface only; that sickness is not in you; you are real being, and in real being perfect health reigns absolutely and eternally. The sickness that sometimes appears in the body is the result of a recognition of untruth, either expressed in wrong thinking or wrong living. Right thought, that is, that thought that invariably follows the recognition of absolute truth, would not produce sickness; and no person could become sick that is always filled and protected with the power of right thought. When the light reigns supremely, darkness cannot enter. Wrong thought comes from a false conception of yourself, and false conceptions will continue to form in mind so long as you are ignorant of the truth. When you know the truth, that you are the image of God, perfect in your own true being, you will think this truth and all your thought will; consequently, only right conditions can exist in your life, and all will henceforth be well with you. When you see yourself as you are in your true being, that you are even now strong and well, in full possession of peace, love, power, wisdom, freedom and all the good that is in God, you will think of yourself accordingly and such thought is right thought. The result will be right conditions in mind and body. From center to circumference your entire being will be well and perfect, as it always was and ever will be in the truth. To think the absolute truth at first seems a contradiction of known facts, because we are so used to judging from appearances, but when we find that appearances are simply the result of thought, that right thought produces good appearances, and wrong thought produces adverse appearances, and learn that true being is the image of God, we shall no longer see contradiction in thinking absolute truth. When we think the truth about ourselves we shall always think the truth about others; we shall, therefore, not think of them as they appear on the surface but as they are in the perfection of real spiritual being. We shall overlook, forgive and forget the wrong appearance, knowing that it is but a temporary effect of wrong thought, and we shall proceed to inspire everyone to change that appearance by thinking right thought, the thought of truth.

7. Live in the spirit. To express this statement in its simplest terms, we would say that to live in the spirit is to live in the upper story of mind and thought, or to live on the good side, the bright side and the true side of everything. To the beginner this is sufficient, because this simple change in living must come before the higher spiritual consciousness can be realized; but the change though simple at first will completely revolutionize life. Ere long, however, the consciousness of the true side and the better side will become so clear that to live in the spirit will mean infinitely more than to simply dwell in the upper story of mind, and when this larger experience comes we shall know from our own illumined understanding what it means to live in the spirit. When we begin to think the truth all kinds of illusions and false beliefs will gradually vanish, and we shall not only understand that we are spiritual beings, but we shall feel that we are all that divine life can be. We shall positively know that we are eternal souls living in a spiritual world now, expressing ourselves in a physical world, and we shall realize that we are actually created in the image and likeness of the Infinite, united with the Infinite and living in the life of Infinite being. Through the fuller realization of truth we will learn that the spiritual is not some vague, far away something that saints alone can know, but that spirit is the essence of all things, the very life of all things visible and invisible, and that spirit is in itself absolutely good and perfect. We will realize that there is but one substance from which all things proceed and that substance is the expression of spirit; we will see that there is but one life, the spiritual life, and that there is but one law, the eternal coming forth in a greater and greater measure of life. We will find that spirit is the basis of all things, the soul of all things, and that therefore all things are in reality very good and very beautiful. We will find through the spirit that evil is but a temporary condition produced by man's understanding of the goodness and the completeness of real being and that to so live that we realize the absolute goodness and the perfect harmony of the whole universe is to live in the spirit. When we realize this we are on the true side of all things and we feel that we are. When we are in harmony with all things we are in harmony with the Infinite and can feel His presence always; and we also find that to "dwell in the secret places of the Most High" is to realize that we are in that great sea of life, the great spiritual sea, the universal state of being, the world of divine existence. While we are in this upper state, that is, in the spirit,

we are away from the false, and actually in the true. We are in the spirit, and from the light of the spirit we can see clearly the truth concerning everything.

From this place we may ascend to other and greater heights and enter into the ever increasing realms of life where existence becomes fairer and higher, too beautiful for tongue to ever describe. What is held in store for the soul that lives in the spirit, eternity alone can reveal, but that the life that is lived in the spirit is the only true life thousands have learned, both in this age and in ages gone by. To the beginner, however, the first essential is to get away from material life, that is, the common, the gross, the superficial, the ordinary, the perverted and the wrong; then to go up higher, to enter the world of light and live in the more beautiful realms of sublime existence. To live in the spirit, live in the highest and most perfect state now, and do not for a moment come down. At first this state will simply be a life that is finer, larger and more harmonious, where things move more smoothly and where the value of life seems to constantly increase; but ere long living in the spirit will mean far more than merely a pleasing state of existence, and the further we advance the more this wonderful life will be, until we begin to understand the great soul who declared: "Eye hath not seen nor ear heard, neither hath it entered into the heart of man what God has prepared for them that love Him." In this connection we must bear in mind that it is not necessary to reach the supreme heights in spiritual life before we can live in the spirit. We can live in the spirit no matter where we may be in the scale of life, because the spiritual life has just as many degrees as there are human souls. Live in the realization that this universe has soul, that this soul is divine, and that you live and move and have your being in that great soul. Realize this as fully as your present state of development will permit, and you have begun to live in the spirit.

The realization of the divinity of the soul side of all things will reveal to your mind the great truth that all things are perfect in their real state of being, and that the real of everything lives in a universe of spirit, a universe that is everywhere within us all and about us all. However, before we begin we must be convinced of the great truth that the spiritual life is not mere sentiment nor a mere feeling of mind and soul. The spiritual life is the real life, the foundation of all life, the essence of all life, the soul of all life, and every true statement concerning the spiritual life is an exact scientific fact readily demonstrated by anyone who will apply the principle. And happy is the soul that does apply this principle, for such a soul will find life in the spirit, not only to be real, but to be infinitely more perfect, more wonderful and more beautiful than anyone has ever dreamed.

The First Steps in Ideal Living

Give your best to the world no matter how insignificant that best may be, and the world will invariably give its best to you. There was nothing great or remarkable about the widow's mite, but it did produce remarkable results, and the reason was she gave her very best. When we give our best we not only receive the best in return from the outer world, but we also receive the best from the inner world. When you give your best you bring forth your best, and it is the bringing forth of your best that causes you to become better and better. When you become better you will meet better people and enter into better environments, and everything in your life will change for the better, because like does attract like. To give much is to become much, provided we give our best and give with the heart. The giving that comes simply from the hand does not count, no matter how large it may be. It brings nothing back to us nor does it bring permanent good to anybody else. When you give your best you do not give from your oversupply or from that which you cannot use. If you have something that you cannot use, it does not belong to you, and you cannot give, in the true sense of the term, what is not your own. To give does not mean simply to give money, unless that is the best you have; but rather to give your own service, your own talents, your ability, your own true worth and your own real self. The man who lives a real life at all times and under all circumstances is giving his best and the very best possible that can be given. A real life truly lived in the world is a power, and the person who lives such a life is a power for good wherever he may be. The presence of such a person is an inspiration and a light, as we all know. The man who loves the whole world with heart and soul, and loves without ceasing is doing far more for the race than he who endows universities, and will receive a far greater reward. We must remember, however, that such a love is not mere sentiment. Real love is a power and will cause the person who has it to do his very best for everybody under every possible circumstance. That person whose heart is with the race will never be satisfied with inferior work. He will never shirk nor leave the problems of life to somebody else; he will go in and push wherever something good is being done, and he will constantly endeavor to render better and better service where ever his field of action may be Such a person will give his best to the world, whether he gives through the channels of art or mechanics, music or literature, physical labor or intellectual labor, ideas or real living. What he does will be the best, and what he receives in return will be the best that the world is able to give. Give the best that you are through every thought, word and deed; that is the principle; and your life will be constantly enriched both from without and from within. Through the daily application of this principle you will develop superiority in mind, soul, character and life, and the world will be better off because you are here.

Expect the best from everybody and everybody will do their best for you. There may be occasional exceptions to this rule, but through close examination we shall find that these exceptions are due solely to our own negligence in applying the law to every occasion. The man who expects the best from everybody and has faith in everybody will certainly receive more love, more kindness, better friendship, better service and more agreeable associates by far than the one who has little or no faith in anyone. But, our faith in people must be alive, and our expectations must have soul. To live constantly in the fear that people will do this or that, and that such and such mistakes may be made, is to live in a confused mental world, and where there is much confusion there will be many mistakes. Mental states are contagious; how that can be is not a matter for present discussion, but the fact that they are is extremely important, and we all know that they are; therefore, if we live in fear and confusion we will be a disturbing element among all those with whom we associate, and if our associates are not mentally strong and positive, they will be more or less confused by our presence, and they are very liable to produce the very mistakes we feared. On the other hand, when we have faith in people we help them to have faith in themselves, and the more faith a person has in himself the fewer his mistakes and the better his work. When we have faith in everybody and are constantly expecting the best from everybody we create wholesome conditions in our own minds, conditions that will tend to develop the best in ourselves; that person, however, who has no faith in others will soon lose faith in himself, and when he does there will be a turn for the worse in his life. True, he may continue to possess a mechanical self confidence or an exaggerated state of egotism, but such a state will soon produce a reaction, and failure will follow. The self confidence that brings out the best that is within us is always founded upon a living faith in the inherent greatness of man; therefore, no one can have real faith in himself unless he also has faith in the greater possibilities of the race, and no one can expect the best from himself and give soul to that expectation unless he also expects the best from others. This is a scientific fact that anyone can prove in his own daily experience. To expect the best from everybody will cause everybody to do their best for you. Look for the best everywhere and you will find the best wherever you go. Why this is so is a matter upon which many delight to speculate, but the why does not concern us just now. It is the fact that this law works that concerns us, and concerns us very much. Not everybody can fully understand why the best is always found by him who never looks for anything but the best, but everybody can look for the best everywhere and thereby find the best; and it is the finding of the best that attracts our attention. It is real results that we are looking for, and the simpler the method the better. The man who will constantly apply this law will not remain in undesirable environments very long, nor will he occupy an inferior position very long; better things will positively come his way and he will not have to wait an age for the change. The man who looks for the best is constantly thinking about the best and constantly impressing his mind with the best thought about everything; and since man is as he thinks we can readily understand why such a man will become better and better; therefore, by looking for the best everywhere he will not only find the best in the external world, but he will create the best in his mental world; this will give him a greater mind, which in turn will produce higher attainments and greater achievements. That man, however, who is always looking for the worst will constantly think about the worst and will fill his mind with inferior thoughts; that he, himself, will become inferior by such a process is a foregone conclusion. We shall positively find, sooner or later, what we constantly look for; it is, therefore, profitable to look for the best everywhere and at all times; we become like those things that we constantly and deeply think about;

it is, therefore, profitable to think only of the best whatever may come or not. The average person may not find the best the very first day this principle is applied. Most of us have strayed so far away from this mode of thinking and living that it may take some time to get back to the path that leads to the best; but one thing is certain, whoever will look for the best everywhere, and continue to do so for a reasonable length of time, will find that path; besides, he will have more delightful experiences while he is training himself to apply this principle than he has had for any similar period before. This, however, will be only the beginning; the future has far greater things in store, if he will continue to look for the best and never look for anything else.

When things are not to your liking, like them as they are. In other words, while you are working for greater things make friends with the lesser things, and they will help you to reach your goal. The person who is dissatisfied with things as they are and discontented because things are not to his liking is standing in his own way. We cannot get away from present conditions so long as we antagonize those conditions, because we are held in bondage to that which we resist. If you want present conditions to become stepping stones to better things, you must get on the better side of present conditions, and you do that by liking things as they are while they remain with you. We must be in harmony with the present if we wish to advance, because in order to advance we must use the present, but we cannot use that with which we are not in harmony. This is a fact that deserves the most thorough attention and will, when understood, explain fully why the average person seems powerless to rise above his surroundings. We must be on friendly terms with everything that exists in our present world if we wish to gain possession of all the building material that our present world can give, and we cannot secure too much material if we desire to build a larger life and a greater future. That which we dislike becomes detrimental to us, no matter how good it may be; nevertheless, it will always be with us because it is impossible to eliminate permanently that which we antagonize; when we run away from it in one place we shall meet it elsewhere in some other form; but that which we love will constantly serve us and help us on to greater things; when it can serve us no longer it will disappear. To like those things, however, that are not to our liking may seem difficult, but the question is why they are not to our liking; when we know that everything in our present world is a stepping stone to something still better it will be natural for us to like everything. Those things may not come up to our ideals, but that is not their real purpose;

it is not the mission of present things to serve as ideals, their mission is to help us to reach our ideals, and they positively can do this if we will take them into friendly cooperation. When you take a drive to an ideal country place you do not dislike the horse because he is not that country place; if you are humane, you will love that horse because he is willing and able to take you where you wish to go. If you should dislike and mistreat that horse or should fail to hitch him to the vehicle, you would not reach your destination. This, however, is the very thing that the average person does with the things of his present world; these things are the horses and the vehicles that can take us to the ideal places we desire to reach; but we must hitch them up; we must treat them right and use them. To cause all things that are about us now to work together with us, we must be in perfect harmony with them; we must like them as they are, and that becomes comparatively easy when we know that it is necessary for them to be what they are in order that they may serve as our stepping stones; if they were different there would be no stepping stones, and we would have to remain where we are. When we realize that everything that exists in our present world has the power to promote our advancement, if we properly use that power, and when we realize that it is necessary to be in harmony with all things to use the power that is within those things, we shall no longer dislike anything; we shall even make friends with adversity, because the power that is in adversity can be tamed by kindness and love; and when that power is tamed it becomes our own. These are great facts and easily demonstrated by anyone, and whoever will apply these principles will find that by liking everything that be finds he will secure the cooperation of everything, and anyone can move forward rapidly when all things are working with him; consequently, by liking what he finds he will find what he likes.

When you do not get what you want take what you can get and call it good. It is better to have something than nothing; besides, we must use what we can get before we can become so strong and so able that we can get whatever we may want. When a person fails to realize his ideals, there is a reason; usually the cause is this: he simply longs for the ideal but does not work himself up to the ideal. And to work himself up to the ideal he needs everything that he can get and use now; by taking what he can get he secures something to work with in promoting his present progress, and by looking upon this something as good he will turn it to good account. It is a well known fact that we get the best out of everything when we meet everything in the conviction that it is good for something, because this attitude invariably brings the mind into conscious touch with the real value of that which is met. What we constantly look for we are sure to find, therefore, by calling everything good that we get and by constantly looking for the real worth of that which we get, the good in everything that we get will be found; the result is that everything we receive or come in contact with will be good for something to us and will have something of value to give us. Gradually, the good will so accumulate that we shall have all that we want; life will be filled with that which has quality and worth, which means that the development towards greater worth will constantly take place, and development towards greater worth means the constant ascension into the realization of our ideals. By accepting and using the good that we can now secure we add so much to the worth of our own life that we become worthy of the greater good we may desire; in consequence, we shall positively receive it. This process may not satisfy those who expect to reach the top at once or expect to receive the better without making themselves better, but it will satisfy those who would rather move forward gradually and surely than stand empty handed waiting and waiting for ages hoping that some miraculous secret may be found through which everything can be accomplished at once. The idea, however, is not that we should meekly submit to things as they are and be satisfied with what little fate may seem willing to give us; that is the other extreme and is just as detrimental to human welfare. Take everything that legitimately comes your way; do not refuse it because it seems too small; take it and call it good, because it is good for something; then make the best possible use of it with a view of getting greater good through that use; expect everything to multiply in your hands; have that faith; accept little things, as well as large things in that conviction, and every good that you do accept will be instrumental in bringing greater good to you. To live in the attitude of turning everything to good account has a most wholesome effect upon mind and character, because that mental attitude will tend to turn everything within yourself to good account; the result will be the constant development of a finer character and a more capable mind. By combining all the results from this mode of living and by noting the greater results that will invariably come from these combined results we must conclude that the total gain will be great, and that he who turns to good account everything that comes into his life, will positively receive everything that be may required to live an ideal life.

Live in the cheerful world, even if you have to create such a world in your own imagination. Resolve to be happy regardless of what comes;

you cannot afford to be otherwise. Count everything joy; meet everything in the spirit of joy, and expect everything to give you joy. By creating a cheerful world in your own imagination you develop the tendency to a sunny disposition, and by meeting everything in the attitude of joy you will soon meet only those things that naturally produce joy. Like does attract like. Much sunshine will gather more sunshine, and the happiest mind meets the most delightful experiences. When exceptions occur pass them by as of no consequence, because they are of no consequence to you; you are interested only in happy events; it is only such events that you desire to meet; therefore, there is no reason whatever why you should pay any attention to the other kind. It is a fact that the less attention we pay to unpleasant conditions the less unpleasantness we meet in life. That person who looks for the disagreeable everywhere and expects to find it everywhere will certainly find what he is looking for in most places, if not in all places. On the other hand, the person who expects only the pleasant will seldom find anything else. We attract what we think of the most. There is no better medicine than cheerfulness, especially for the circulation and the digestive functions. Keep your mind full of living joy and your circulation will be strong in every part of your being, and a strong full circulation is one of the secrets to perfect health. Another great secret to health is a good digestion, and it is well to remember that so long as you are thoroughly bright and happy you can digest almost anything. The greatest value of cheerfulness, however, is found in its effect upon the mind; that is, in its power to make faculties and talents grow, just as sunshine makes flowers grow. It is a well known fact that the most cheerful mind is the most brilliant mind, other things being equal, and that the brightest ideas always come when you are in the brightest frame of mind. This makes cheerfulness indispensable to those who wish to improve themselves and develop superior mental power. The depressed mind is always dull and never sees anything clearly; while the cheerful mind learns more readily, remembers more easily and understands more perfectly; but we must not conclude that cheerfulness is all that is necessary to the development of a fine intelligence; there must be mental power and mental quality as well; but the power and the quality of the mind, however great, cannot be fully expressed without an abundance of mental sunshine. Though the warmest sunshine may fail to make a gravel knoll productive, still the most fertile soil will remain barren so long as the sunshine is absent. There are thousands of fertile minds in the world that are almost wholly unproductive, because they lack mental sunshine. If these would cultivate real genuine mental brightness every part of the world would sparkle with brilliant ideas. What the acorn is to the oak bright ideas are to a great and successful life, and we all can produce bright ideas through the development of mental ability and the cultivation of mental sunshine. Cheerfulness keeps the body in the best condition and brings out the best that there is in the mind. To attain the cheerful state we must remember that it is a product of the inner life and does not come from circumstances or conditions; therefore, the first essential is to create a cheerful world in the imagination; picture in mind the brightest states of existence that you can think of and impress joy upon mind at all times; feel joy, think joy, and make every action of mind and body thrill with joy; ere long you will have created within yourself the subconscious cause of joy, and when this is done cheerfulness and brightness will become permanent elements in yourself.

Live in the present only, and seek to make the great eternal now as full and complete as possible. It is what we do for the present that counts; the past is gone, and the future is not ready to be acted upon. Give your time, your talent and your power to that which is now at hand and you will do things worth while, you will not waste thought upon what you expect to do, but you will turn all your energies upon that which you now can do; results will positively follow. The man who does things worth while in the present will not have to worry about the future; for such a man the future has rich rewards in abundance. The greater the present cause the greater the future effect. Nine tenths of the worries in the average life are simply about the future; all of these will be eliminated when we learn to live in the present only. Instead of giving anxious thought to the bridge we may have to cross we should give scientific thought to the increase of present ability and power; thus we make ourselves fully competent to master every occasion that we may meet. To judge the present. The present moment should be dealt cause if we are advancing, the present is not only larger than the past, but quite different in many if not all respects. To follow the past is to limit one's self to the lesser accomplishments of the past and thus prevent the very best from being attained in the present. The present moment should be dealt with according to the needs of the present moment regardless of what was done under similar conditions in the past. There is sufficient wisdom at hand now to solve all the problems of the present moment, if we will make full, practical application of that wisdom. He who lives for the present only will live a larger life, a happier life, a far more useful life; this is perfectly natural, because he will not scatter his forces over past ages and future ages, but will concentrate his whole life, all his power, all his ability upon that which he is trying to do now; he will be his best today, because he will give all of his best to the life of today, and he who is his best today will be still better tomorrow.

Never complain, criticize or condemn, but meet all things in a constructive attitude of mind. The critical mind is destructive to itself, and will in time become wholly incompetent to even produce logical criticism. To complain about everything is to constantly think about the inferior side of everything, thus impressing inferiority upon the mind; this will cause the entire process of thinking to become inferior; in consequence, the retrogression of the man himself will inevitably follow. Refuse to complain about anything; complaints never righted a wrong and never will. When you seek to gain justice through complaint you temporarily gain something in one place and permanently lose something in another; besides, you have harmed your own mind. The fact is that the more you complain the worse things will become; and the more you criticize what you meet today the more adverse and inferior will be the things you are to meet tomorrow. The reason why is simple; the complaining mind attracts the cheap and the common, and the critical spirit goes directly down into weakness and inferiority. However, we must remember in this connection that there is a marked difference between the critical attitude and the discriminating attitude. When things are not right we should say so, but while saying so we should not enter into a "rip and tear" frame of mind; the facts should be stated firmly but gently and without the slightest trace of ill feeling or condemnation; simply discriminate between the white and the black and state the facts, but let no hurt whatever appear in your voice. What we say is important, but the way things are said is far more important; even truth itself, can be expressed in such a way that it hurts, harms and destroys; this, however, is not true expression. It is truth misdirected, and always produces undesirable effects. To state your wants in a friendly manner is not complaint, but when there are hurts and whines in your voice you are making complaints and you are harming yourself; besides, you are producing unfavorable impressions upon those with whom you come in contact. It is far better to have faith in people than to criticize and complain, even though everything seems to go wrong, because when we have faith in people we shall finally attract those who are after our own hearts, and who are competent to do things the way we wish to have them done. Instead of complaining, or stating that there is always something wrong, we should live constantly in the strong faith that everything is eternally coming right; we thus place ourselves in harmony with those laws that can and will make things right. This is no idle dream, nor shall we have to wait a long time to secure results. The very day we establish faith in the place of complaints, criticisms and distrust, the tide will turn; things will change for the better in our world, and continue to improve perpetually.

Make the best use of every occasion, and nothing but opportunities will come your way. He who makes the best of everything will attract the best of everything, and it is always an opportunity to meet the best. There are occasions that seem worthless, and the average person thinks he is wasting time while he is passing through such states, but no matter how worthless the occasion may seem to be the one who makes the best use of it while he is in it will get something of real value out of it; in addition, the experience will have exceptional worth, because whenever we try to turn an occasion to good account we turn everything in ourselves to good account. The person who makes the best use of every occasion is developing his mind and strengthening his own character every day; to such a person every occasion will become an opportunity and will consequently place him in touch with the greater world of opportunities. Much gathers more and many small opportunities will soon attract a number of larger ones; then comes promotion, advancement and perpetual increase. "To him that hath shall be given." Every event has the power to add to your life, and will add to your life, if you make the best use of what it has to give; this will constantly increase the power of your life, which will bring you into greater occasions and better opportunities than, you ever knew before. Make the best use of everything that comes your way; greater things will positively follow; that is the law, and he who daily applies this law has a brilliant future before him.

Never antagonize anything, neither in thought, word nor deed, but live in that attitude that is non resisting to evil while positively and continuously inclined towards the good. You give your energy to that which you resist; you thereby give life to the very thing you seek to destroy. To resist evil is to increase the power of evil, and at the same time take life and power away from that good which you wish to develop or promote. The antagonistic mind develops bitterness in itself and thereby becomes just as disagreeable as the thing disliked; frequently more so, and we cannot expect to be drawn into the more delightful elements of the ideal while we ourselves are becoming less and less ideal. To live in the antagonistic attitude is to perpetuate a destructive process throughout mind and body, and at the same time suffer a constant loss of energy. We therefore cannot afford to be antagonistic at any time, nor even righteously indignant, no matter how perfectly in the right we may be; though in this connection it is well to remember that indignation never can be righteous. There are a number of minds that have the habit of feeling an inner bitterness towards those beliefs or systems of thought which they cannot accept. Frequently there can be no logical grounds for such a feeling. In many instances it is simply hereditary, or the result of foundationless prejudice; nevertheless, it is there and is actually sapping life and power out of the mind that has it. This habit is therefore responsible for much mental weakness, inability and consequent failure; and as everything that tends to decrease the life and the power of the individual tends to shorten his life, as well as decrease the value and usefulness of his life, it is evident that we cannot afford to feel bitter toward any religion, any belief, any doctrine, any party or any person whatever; we harm ourselves by so doing and do not add to the welfare or happiness of anybody. Be on friendly terms with the entire universe and feel kindly towards every creature in existence; leave the ills of perverted life to die; let the "dead bury their dead." It is our privilege to press on and promote the greatest good that we know; and when we give our whole time and attention to the highest attainment of the greatest good, evil will die of itself. This is what it means to overcome evil with good, and it is the one perfect path to complete emancipation, both for the individual and for the race. If you wish to serve the race do not antagonize systems, doctrines, methods or beliefs; be an inspiration to the race by actually doing the very best you know now.

The First Thought In Ideal Thinking

But seek ye first his kingdom, and his righteousness; and all these things shall be added unto you. Mat. 6: 33.

The kingdom of God is a spiritual kingdom within man and manifests through man as the spiritual life. His righteousness is the right use of all that is contained in the elements of the spiritual life. The spiritual life being the complete life, the full expression of life in body, mind and soul, it is evident that the right use of the spiritual life will produce and bring everything that man may need or desire. The source of everything has the power to produce everything, provided the power within that source is used according to exact spiritual law. The spiritual life being the source of all that is necessary to a full and perfect life, and the kingdom within being the source of the spiritual life, we can readily understand why the kingdom should be sought first; and also why everything that we may require will be added when the first thought is given to spiritual living, ideal thinking and righteous action. Righteous action, however, does not simply imply moral action, but the right use of the elements of life in all action.

The kingdom of God is the spiritual side of all things. This spiritual side is within the manifested or visible side; that is, everything is filled with an inner, finer something that is perfect and complete. Every part of the outer world is filled and permeated with an inner world, and everything that appears in the outer world is a partial manifestation or expression of what exists in a perfect and complete state in the inner world. This inner world is the kingdom referred to, and as it is inexhaustible in every sense of that term, there is nothing we cannot receive when we learn to draw upon the riches of this vast inner realm. In the life of man we have the outer and the inner worlds; the personal life in the without and the great spiritual life in the within. What appears in the outer world of man, that is, in his personal existence, is the result of what he has sought and brought forth from his inner world. According to one of the greatest of metaphysical laws we express whatever we become conscious of. We, therefore, understand clearly why the personal man, or his outer world, is the direct result of what he has become conscious of in his interior world. Man is what he is in the without, because he has sought the corresponding elements in the within, and he may change the without in any manner desired by seeking first in the within those qualities and attributes that he may desire.

To seek and find the within is to become conscious of the within, and what is thus sought and found will express itself in personal life; but its real value will depend upon whether it is properly used or not. To seek the richer kingdom within is the first essential, but to promote the righteous use of these greater riches is the second essential, and is just as important as the first. To give the first thought at all times to the great spiritual kingdom within, it is not necessary to withdraw attention from the outer world nor to deny one's self the good things that may exist in the outer world. To seek the kingdom first is to give one's strongest thought to the spiritual life, and to make spiritual thought the predominating thought in everything that one may do in life; in other words, live so closely to the spiritual kingdom within that you are fully conscious of that kingdom every moment, and depend absolutely upon supreme power to carry you through whatever you may undertake to do. To seek the kingdom first the heart must be in the spirit; that is, to live in the full realization of the inner spiritual life at all times must be the one predominating desire. However, the mental conception of the spiritual life must not be narrow, but must contain the perfection of everything that can possibly appear in life.

To think of the spiritual life as being distinct from mind and body, is to prevent the elements of the great interior life from being expressed in mind and body, and what is not expressed cannot be lived. The spiritual life in this larger sense must be thoroughly lived in mind and body. The power of the spiritual must be made the soul of all power, and the law of spiritual action must be made the rule and the guide in all action. When the spiritual is lived in all life the richness and the quality and the worth of the spiritual will be expressed in all life, and spiritual worth means the sum total of all worth. There are any number of minds in the world who now realize this greater worth and who have found the spiritual riches within to an extraordinary degree, but they have not in every instance sought righteousness; therefore, these spiritual riches have been of no use; frequently they have become obstacles in the living of a life of personal welfare and growth.

Real righteousness means right living and exact scientific thinking; that is, the correct expression of everything of which we are now conscious. To be righteous does not simply mean to be moral and truthful and just, but to live in harmony with all laws, physical, mental, moral and spiritual. To be in harmony with physical law, is to adapt one's self orderly to everything in the external world; to resist no exterior force, but to constructively use every exterior force in such a manner that perpetual physical development may take place. To be in harmony with mental laws is to promote scientific thinking; that is, to think the truth about everything and to see everything from the universal viewpoint. Scientific thinking is that mode of thinking that causes all the forces of mind and thought to constantly work for greater things. To be in harmony with moral laws is to live a life of complete purity; and purity in the true sense of the term is the doing of all things at the right time, in the right place and with the right motive; in other words, every action is a pure action that leads to higher and better things. All other actions are not pure, therefore not moral. To be in harmony with spiritual laws is to live in constant conscious touch with the inner or higher side of everything. To apply the spiritual law is to seek the spiritual first, no matter what the goal in view may be; to seek first the spiritual counterpart that is within everything, to make the spiritual thought the predominating thought and to dwell constantly in the spiritual attitude. We enter the spiritual attitude when we enter the upper story of the mind and mentally face that supreme side of life that is created in the likeness of the Supreme. Briefly stated, to be righteous is to be in harmony with the outer side of life, to think the truth, to live in real purity, to dwell on the spiritual heights and to give full and complete expression to the highest and the best of which we are now conscious. When this is done we shall rightly manifest whatever we may find in the kingdom within. Righteousness, however, is not a definite goal but a perpetual process of attainment that involves the entire being of man. The righteous man is right and perfect as far as he has ascended in the scale of life at present, though not simply in a moral sense, but in every sense, including body, mind and soul.

The righteous man is never weak, never sick, and is never in a state of discord or disorder. This is a great truth that we should not fail to remember. Sickness, weakness, discord and all other adverse conditions come from the violation of law somewhere in human life, but the righteous man violates no law. He is true to life as far as he has ascended in the scale of life. To be righteous in the absolute sense of the term is to use everything in our present world as God uses everything in His world, which means in harmony with its own nature, in harmony with its sphere of action, and in harmony with that law that leads upward and onward forever. Righteous action is that action that is always harmonious and that always works for better things, greater things, higher things. The great majority of those minds that are awakened to the reality of the spiritual side of things have already found an abundance of good things in the vast interior life that is ready for manifestation in personal life, but as most of these have neglected the law of real righteousness this abundance remains inactive in the potential state and all other things as promised are not added. That all other things will be added when His kingdom and His righteousness are sought first may not seem clear to everybody, because the kingdom of God has been looked upon as a far away place that we are to enter when we leave the body, and righteousness has been looked upon as simply a moral, just and honest mode of living. But when we realize that the kingdom is the great spiritual world within us, and that from this world comes all wisdom, all power, all talent, all life; in brief, everything that we now possess in body, mind and soul, and that everything we are to receive in the future must come from the same source, we understand clearly why the kingdom must be sought first.

We cannot secure anything unless we go to the source, and the spiritual kingdom within us is the one only source of everything that is manifested in human life. When we desire more wisdom and a greater understanding it is evident that we can obtain these things only by entering real mental light, and that light is within us in the spirit. By entering into the consciousness of the illumined world within we naturally receive more light. We ourselves, become illumined to a degree, frequently to a great degree, and we thus gain the power to understand perfectly what we could neither desire nor comprehend before. When we seek more life and power we can find the greater life only in the eternal life, and the eternal life is the life of the spirit in the kingdom within.

"They that wait upon the Lord shall renew their strength." To wait upon the Lord is to enter into the spiritual presence of the Infinite, and whenever we enter into the presence of the Infinite we enter into the life of the Infinite and we are thus filled through and through with the supreme power of that life. When we enter into the spiritual kingdom within we enter into the Christ consciousness and in that consciousness we receive the life more abundant, because to be in the Christ consciousness is to be in the very spirit of the limitless life of the Christ. When we seek health we can find it in the kingdom, because in the spirit all is always well. There is a realm within man where perfect health reigns supremely and eternally. In that realm everything is always perfectly whole and to enter into that realm is to enter into absolute health and wholeness. No one who lives constantly in the spirit can possibly be sick, because sickness can no more enter the spiritual state than darkness can enter where there is absolute light. To enter the kingdom within is to enter health, happiness and harmony in the highest, largest degree; therefore, by seeking the kingdom, health will be added, happiness will be added, harmony will be added. It is impossible, however, to gain health, happiness and harmony, in the true sense, from any other source. But to seek these qualities in the kingdom is not sufficient. We must also seek righteousness or the right expressions of those things. If we misuse any organ, faculty, function or power anywhere in body, mind or soul, we cannot remain in health, no matter how spiritual we may try to be.

To enter the kingdom within is to enter the perpetual increase of power, because there is no limit to the power of the spirit, and the more power we enter into or become conscious of the more power we shall give to mind and body; in consequence, the more spiritual we become the stronger we become, the more able we become, the more competent we become and the more we can accomplish whatever our work may be; and he who can do good work in the world invariably receives the good things of the world. To his life will be added all those things that can make personal existence rich and beautiful. To enter the kingdom within is to enter the life of freedom. There is no bondage in the spirit, and as we grow in the spirit we grow out of every form of bondage. One adverse condition after another disappears until absolute freedom is gained. Therefore, when we seek first His kingdom and His righteousness we shall find the life of complete emancipation. Perfect freedom in all things and at all times will positively be added.

There are thousands of aspiring souls in this age that are trying to develop their powers and talents so that they might be of greater use in the world, but if these would seek the kingdom first, they would find within themselves the real source of every talent; and as the only way to permanently increase anything is to increase the expressions of its source we understand perfectly why greatness can come only when we begin to live in the great within. We must always bear in mind that what we become conscious of we bring forth into personal expression, but we cannot become conscious of the larger source of any quality or talent unless we enter into the spirit of that quality and talent, and as the spirit of all things has its source of real existence in the kingdom within, we must enter this interior world if we wish to become conscious of a larger and a larger measure of those things that we wish to express.

That any person can improve his environment or overcome poverty by seeking the kingdom first may not seem possible, but the truth is that adverse conditions will positively disappear after one begins to actually live the full spiritual life. Poverty has two causes; lack of ability and the misplacing of ability. To improve ability to any degree the within must be awakened. We must learn to draw upon the inexhaustible sources of the inner life and become conscious of the greater capacity that lies latent within us. This is accomplished by seeking the kingdom first. By giving your first thought, your predominating thought to the great and mighty world within, your mind will gradually enter more deeply into the life of this inner world. You thus become conscious of the larger powers within, because consciousness always follows the predominating thought. What you think of the most develops in yourself. When you think the most of the spiritual, consciousness will follow your spiritual thought and thus enter more deeply into the spirit. The result is you become conscious of a larger spiritual domain every day, you become conscious of a greater capacity within yourself every day, and since you always express what you become conscious of you will cause greater ability and capacity to be developed and expressed in yourself every day; you thereby remove the first cause of poverty and place yourself in a position where you will be in greater demand, and the greater the demand for your service the greater will be your recompense.

There are a number of people who have misplaced their talents that may have considerable ability, but they are not in the work for which they are adapted, and therefore do not succeed. They may have been forced into their present positions by necessity, or they may have chosen their present places through inferior judgment, but both of these causes may be changed by seeking the kingdom first. When we enter the spiritual everything clears up. We not only see our mistakes, but also how to correct them; therefore, if you are in the wrong place, enter the spiritual light of the kingdom within, and you will see clearly where you belong. If you do not know whether you are in the proper sphere or not, enter the spirit. Constantly live in the spirit and you will soon know; you will also know when and how to change. By entering this state where the outlook is infinitely greater you will see opportunities, open doors, possibilities, and pastures green that you never saw before; and you will also see clearly which one you have the power and the capacity to take advantage of now. If you have been forced into the wrong place by necessity, the larger mental life that will come when you seek the kingdom will give you the power to command something better, and the superior wisdom that comes through the light of the spirit will guide you in your choice. Instead of adversity and constant need you will have peace, harmony and abundance. You will pass from the world of poverty and limitations to a world that can offer a future as brilliant as the sun.

The man who fights adversity and complains of his lot will continue in poverty and need. He will remain in mental darkness; he will be daily misled, and will always be doing the wrong thing at the wrong time. Such a life breeds ill luck and misfortune and perpetuates the poverty that already exists. However, let this person enter into harmony with his present fate, count everything joy, and realize that he can make his present misfortune a stepping stone to better things; then let him give his first thought to the kingdom, to the greater life and power and capacity within, to the superior creative powers of his own mind, those powers that are able even now to create for him a better fate, if he will but place before them a better pattern; the results will be peace of mind first, then hope of the better, then the vision of great changes near at hand, then the faith that the new life, the new time and the better days are now being created for his world. And when a person begins to inwardly feel that things are taking a turn, that better days are coming and that the good is beginning to accumulate in his life, the victory is nearly won. A little more faith and perseverance and the crowning day is at hand. From that moment all things will begin to work together for good things and for still greater things, providing the mind is held in constant conscious touch with the spiritual kingdom within, and all the laws of life are employed according to the highest ideal of righteousness.

Many a person, however, has failed while on the very verge of his victory, because he neglected the kingdom when he began to see the change coming. By giving his first thought to the material benefits that he expected to secure, his consciousness is taken away from the spirit and becomes confused in those things that had not as yet been placed in the true order of perpetual increase. The result is a scattering of forces and his loss upon the hold of the good things that were beginning to gravitate towards his world. While ascending this upward path we must at every step keep the eye single upon the kingdom, upon the spiritual, upon the larger and the higher life within. When the other things are being added we must not forget the kingdom and give our first thoughts to the other things. We shall enjoy these other things so much the more, if we continue to give the first thought to the spirit. This is evident, because while giving the first thought to the spirit everything that comes into our world will be spiritualized, refined and perfected, and will thus be given added power and worth. When we continue to give the first thought to the spiritual kingdom those other things that are added will enter our world at their best and we shall thus receive the best that those things may have to give.

We are always at our best when we are on the heights, and we gain the power to create, produce and attract those things from every part of life that correspond to the life on the heights. Therefore, by living on the heights in the spiritual kingdom we gain everything that we may require; we gain the best of everything that we may require, and we are in that condition where we can make the best use of what comes, and enjoy what comes to the highest and most perfect degree. We can thus readily understand that when we seek the kingdom of God constantly, giving our first thought to the spiritual and seeking to live righteously according to this larger view of righteousness, all problems of life will be solved. All the crooked paths of life will be made straight; obstacles will disappear; our circumstances will change to correspond with our ideas, and we will daily enter into a better life and a greater state of existence than we ever knew before. The problems of the world can be solved in the same way. Therefore, the greatest thing that we can do for the human race is to make clear this law, that is, the law through which His kingdom and His righteousness may be sought first by any individual, no matter what the degree of that individual's understanding may be. To promote a real spiritual movement on the largest possible scale is to cause the ills of humanity to gradually, but surely, pass away.

This planet will then become, not a vale of tears, but what it is intended to be, the kingdom of heaven realized upon earth.

The human race, however, is the product of human thought; therefore, the prime essential is to inspire the human mind with the power to give His kingdom and His righteousness the first thought. To make the ideal real upon earth, all thinking must be ideal; and to cause all things to become ideal the foundation of all things must be based upon pure spiritual thought; that is, every thought that is created in the mind must be animated with this great first thought, the thought of the kingdom within and the full righteous expression of that kingdom. When we seek first the kingdom and his righteousness all other things are added, not in some mysterious manner, nor do they come of themselves regardless of conscious effort to work in harmony with the law of life. We receive from the kingdom only what we are prepared to use in the living of a great life and in the doing of great and worthy things in the world. We receive only in proportion to what we give, and it is only as we work well that we produce great results; but by entering the spiritual life we receive everything that we may require in order to give as much as we may desire, to do as much as we may desire. We gain the power and the talent to do everything that is necessary to give worth and superiority to our entire state of existence. When we enter the spiritual life we gain every quality that is necessary in making life full and complete now, and we gain the power to produce and create in the external world whatever we may need or desire. In other words, we receive everything we want from within and we gain the power to produce everything we want in the without. We, therefore, need never take anxious thought about these other things. By seeking first His kingdom and His righteousness we shall positively receive these other things. The way will be open to all that is rich, beautiful and superior in life, and we shall be abundantly supplied with the best that life can give.

The Ideal and the Real Made One

When the elements of the ideal are blended harmoniously with the elements of the real the two become one; the ideal becomes real and the real gives expression to the qualities of the ideal. To be in harmony with everything at all times and under all circumstances is therefore one of the great essentials in the living of that life that is constantly making real a larger and larger measure of the ideal; and so extremely important is continuous harmony that nothing should be permitted to produce confusion or discord for the slightest moment. Discord wastes energy, while harmony accumulates energy. If we wish to be strong in mind and body and do the best possible work, harmony is absolutely necessary and we must be in the best possible condition to make real the ideal. The person who lives in perpetual harmony with everything will accomplish from ten to one hundred per cent more than the average during any given period of time; a fact that gives the elements of harmony a most important place in life. When harmony is absent there is always a great deal of mental confusion, and a confused mind can never think clearly, therefore makes mistakes constantly. To establish complete and continuous mental harmony will reduce mistakes to a minimum in any mind; another fact that makes the attainment of harmony one of the great attainments.

The mind that is living in continuous harmony is realizing a great measure of heaven upon earth regardless of his personal attainments or external possessions. He has made real that ideal something that makes existence thoroughly worth while, and he is rich indeed. To live in harmony is to gain the joy everlasting, the contentment that is based upon the real value of life, and that satisfaction that grows larger and better for every day that passes by. On the other hand, to live in discord is to live in perpetual torment, even though our personal attainments may be great and our personal possessions as large as any mind could wish.

To live the good life, the ideal life, the beautiful life, we must be at peace with all things, including ourselves, and every thought, word and deed must be harmonious. Whatever we wish to do or be it is wisdom to make any sacrifice necessary for the sake of harmony, although that which we sacrifice for the sake of harmony is not a sacrifice. When we enter into harmony we will regain everything that we were willing to lose in order that we might possess harmony. When we establish ourselves in perfect harmony we shall be reunited with everything that we hold near and dear and the new unity will be far sweeter, far more beautiful than the one we had before. "My own shall come to me" is a favorite expression among all those who believe that every ideal can be made real, and many of these are waiting and watching for their own to come, wondering in the meantime what can be done to hasten that coming. There are many things to be done, however, but one of the most important is the attainment of harmony. No person who lives in perpetual harmony will be deprived very long of his own, whatever that own may be. Whatever you deserve, whatever you are entitled to, whatever belongs to you will soon appear in your world, if you are living in perfect harmony.

To enter harmony is to enter a new world where everything is better, where opportunities are greater and more numerous, and where persons, conditions and things are more agreeable. You will not only enter a better world, however, but the attitude of harmony will relate your life so perfectly to the good things in all worlds that may exist about you, that the best from every source will naturally gravitate towards your sphere of existence. But harmony will not only cause the good things of life to gravitate towards you; it will also cause you to radiate the good qualities in your own being and thus become a perpetual benediction to everybody. To be in the presence of a person who dwells serenely in the beautiful calm is, indeed, a privilege, especially to those who can appreciate the finer elements of a truly harmonious life. Whenever we are in touch with real harmony, whether it comes from the music of human life, the music of nature or the music of the spheres, we are one step nearer the Beautiful. We can therefore realize the great value of being able to actually live in perfect harmony at all times. The life of harmony is the foundation of happiness and health and is one of the greatest essentials to achievement and real success. When we look into the past we can always find that our failures originated in confusion; likewise our troubles and ills. On the other hand, all the good things that have happened to us in the past, or that are happening in the present, had their origin and their growth in the elements of continuous harmony; the ideal and the real were made one, and we consequently reached the goals we had in view.

The mind that works in perpetual harmony does more work and far better work than is possible in any other condition; besides, harmonious work is invariably conducive to higher development and growth. To work in harmony is to promote increase and development in all the qualities and powers of the personality; while to work in confusion is to weaken the entire system and thus originate causes that will terminate in failure. The majority state that they have no time for self development, but to live in harmony and work in harmony is to promote self development every moment, and this development will not be confined simply to those muscles or faculties that we use directly, but will express itself throughout the entire system; and the mind especially will, under such conditions, steadily gain both in power and in worth. In the presence of these facts we can realize readily that no person can afford to permit discord, disturbance or confusion at any time. The many declare, however, that they cannot help it, but we must help it and we can. There is no reason why our minds should be excited or our nerves upset at any time. We can prevent this just as easily as we can refuse to eat what we do not want.

To proceed, we must apply exact reason to this great subject. We should learn to understand that no wrong will be righted because we permit ourselves to "fly to pieces;" also that the act of becoming nervous over a trouble will never drive that trouble away. To live in a constant strain will not promote our purpose nor arrange matters the way we want them. This is a fact that we should impress deeply upon our minds, and then impress our minds to take another and a better course. The average person feels that it is a religious duty to be as excited as possible, and to string up all his nerves as high as possible, whenever he is passing through some exceptional event; in consequence, he spoils all or practically all of that which might have been gained; besides, he places his system in a condition where all sorts of ills may gain a foothold. There are many reasons why such a large number of undertakings fail, but one of the principal reasons is found in the fact that few people have learned to retain perfect harmony under all kinds of circumstances. Discord and confusion are usually present to a great degree, and in consequence, something almost invariably goes wrong. But when a person is in perfect harmony and does his very best, he will succeed at least in a measure every time, and he will thus prepare himself for the greater opportunities that are sure to follow: To believe that intelligent, well educated people almost daily break down over mere trifles is not mere simplicity, but the fact that it is the truth leads us to question why. Intelligence and education should give those who possess it the power to know better. Modern education, however, does not teach us how to use ourselves. We have learned how to mix material substances so as to satisfy every imaginable taste, and we have learned how to use the tangible forces of nature so as to construct almost anything we like in the physical world, but we have not learned how to combine the elements of mind so as to produce health, happiness, strength, brilliancy and harmony whenever we may so desire. A few, however, have made the attempt, but the elements of the mind will not combine for greater efficiency and higher states of expression unless the mind is in perfect harmony.

We have all learned to remember, but few have learned to think. To repeat verbatim what others have thought and said is counted knowledge and with such borrowed knowledge the majority imagine they are satisfied, the reason being they have not discovered the art of thinking thoughts of their own. This is an art that every person must learn; the sooner the better, if the ideal is to be made real. Original thinking is the secret of all greatness, all high attainments, all extraordinary achievements and all superior states of being; but no mind can create original thought until a high state of mental harmony is attained. To produce mental harmony we must first bear in mind the great fact that it is not what happens that disturbs us, but the way we think about that which happens; and our thought about anything depends upon our point of view. The way we look at things will determine whether the experience will produce discord or harmony, and it is in our power to look at things in any way that we may desire. When we are face to face with those things that usually upset the mind we should immediately turn our attention upon the life and the power that is back of the disturbing element, having the desire to find the better side of that life and power constantly in view. Everything has its better side, its ideal side, its calm and undisturbed side, and a mere desire to gain a glimpse of that better side will turn the mind away from confusion and cause attention to be centered upon that calm state that is being sought. This will decrease discord at once, and if applied the very moment we are aware of confusion we will entirely prevent any mental disturbance whatever. To meet all circumstances and events in this way is to develop in ourselves a harmonious attitude towards all things, and when we are established in this harmonious attitude nothing whatever disturbs us; no matter what may happen we will continue to remain in harmony, and will consequently be able to deal properly with whatever may happen.

The mind that is upset by confused circumstances will lose ground and fail, but the mind that continues calmly in harmony with everything, no matter what the circumstances may be, will master every occasion and steadily rise in the scale. He will continue to make real the ideal, because he is living in that harmonious state of being where the ideal and the real are harmoniously blended into one. To promote the highest and most perfect state of continuous harmony we must learn to meet those persons, things and events, with which we come in daily contact, in the right mental attitude. The result of such an attitude is determined directly by the nature of our own attitude of mind, and as we can express ourselves through any attitude we desire, it is in our power either to spoil the most promising prospects, or convert the most unpromising conditions into the greatest success. We should train ourselves to meet everything in that attitude of mind that expects all things to work out right. When we deeply and continually expect all things to work out right we relate ourselves more perfectly with that with which we come in contact; we take things, so to speak, the way they ought to be taken, and we thereby promote harmony and cooperation among all things concerned.

Though this be extremely important, it is insignificant, however, in comparison with another great fact in this connection; that is, the way things respond to the leading desires of the ruling mind; whether it is the exercise of the mysteries of mental force or the application of a mental law not generally understood, does not concern us just now; but it is a fact that things will do, as a rule what we persistently expect them to do. To understand why this is so may require some study of the great laws of mind and body, and everybody should seek to understand these laws perfectly; but in the meantime anyone can demonstrate the fact that things will work out right if we constantly expect them to do so. No matter what may happen we should continue in the faith that all things will come right, and as our faith is so it shall be. To place ourselves in perfect harmony with all things, the domineering attitude of mind must be eliminated completely. The mind that tries to domineer over things will not only lose control of things, but will lose control of its own faculties and forces. At first it may seem that the domineering mind gains ground, but the gain is only temporary. When the reaction comes, as it will, the loss will be far greater than the temporary gain. When you try to domineer over persons and things you gain possession and control of those things only that are too weak to control themselves. That is, you gain a temporary control over negatives, and negatives have no permanent value in your life; in fact, they soon prove themselves to be wholly detrimental. Occasionally a domineering mind may attract the attention of better things, but as soon as his domineering qualities are discovered those better things will part company with him at once. The law of attraction is at the foundation of all natural constructive processes; therefore, to promote construction, growth, advancement and real success we must work in harmony with that law. If we wish to attain the superior, we must become superior, because it is only like that attracts like. If we wish to gain the ideal, we must become ideal. If we wish to make real the ideal, we must live the ideal in the real. When you want good things, make yourself better, and better things will naturally be attracted to you; but good things do not submit to force. Therefore, to try to secure better things through forceful methods, or through the domineering attitude can only result in failure; such methods gain only the inferior, those things that can add neither to the welfare nor the happiness of any one. This fact holds good, not only among individuals, but also among nations and institutions. The more domineering an institution is the more inferior are its members, and the more autocratic the nation the weaker its subjects. On the other hand, we find the best minds where the individual is left free to govern himself and where he is expected to act wisely, to be true to the best that is within him. In order that the individual may advance he must steadily grow in the mastery of himself, and must so relate himself to the best things in life that he will naturally attract the best things; but these two essentials are wholly interfered with by the domineering attitude. Such an attitude repels everything and everybody that has any worth. It spoils the forces of mind, thus weakening all the mental faculties, and it steadily undermines whatever self control a person might possess. Never try to control anything or domineer over anything, but aim to live in perpetual harmony with the highest, the truest and the best that is in everything.

Whatever happens we should approach that event in that attitude that believes it is all right. We should never permit the attitude that condemns, not even when the things concerned have proved themselves to be wrong. The attitude that condemns is detrimental to our own minds, because it invariably produces discord. When you meet all things in the expectation of finding them right, you always find something about them that is right. This something you may appropriate and thus gain good from everything that happens. That person, however, who expects to find most things wrong will fail to see the good that may exist among the things that come his way; therefore, he gains far less from life than his wiser neighbor. But what is equally important, the man who expects to find everything right wherever he may go, will gradually gravitate towards those people and circumstances that are right. The man who expects to find everything wrong usually finds what he expects. The effect of these two attitudes upon mind and character is even more important, because the man is as his mind and character, and as the man is so is his destiny. The man who expects to find most things wrong and meets the world in that attitude is constantly impressing the wrong upon his mind, and as we gradually grow into the likeness of that which we think of the most, he is building upon sinking sand. The mind that is constantly looking for the wrong cannot be wholesome. Such a mind is not in harmony with the law of growth, power, and ability; therefore, can never do its best. Unwholesome thoughts will steadily undermine the finest character and mind, and the world is full of illustrations. There is always something wrong in the life of that person who constantly expects to find things wrong, and the reason why is simple. His own expectations are reacting upon himself; by thinking about the wrong he is creating the wrong and thus bringing forth the wrong in every part of his life.

The man, however, who expects to find everything right and meets the world in that attitude is daily nourishing his mind with right thoughts, wholesome thoughts and constructive thoughts; he thinks the most of that which is right, and is therefore steadily growing more and more into the likeness of that which is right, perfect, worthy and good; he is daily changing for the better, and through this constant change he steadily rises in the scale and thereby meets the better and the better at every turn. By expecting to find everything right he finds more and more of that which is right, and as he is becoming stronger in mind, character and soul, he is affected less and less by those few things that may not be as they should be. When you meet a disappointment meet it in the conviction that it is all right, because through this attitude you enter into harmony with the power that is back of the event at hand, and you thus convert the disappointment into a channel through which greater good may be secured. Those who doubt this should try it;

they will find that it is based upon exact scientific facts Transcend disappointment, and all the powers of adversity will begin to rise with you and will begin to work with you and help you reach the goal you have in view. You will thus find that, it is all for the best, because through the right mental attitude you made everything work out in such a way that the best transpired as a final result.

To live in what may be termed the "all right" attitude, that is, in that attitude that expects to find everything all right and that constantly affirms that everything is all right, is to press on to the realization and the possession of those things that are as you wish them to be. Disappointments and failures, when met in this attitude, simply become open doors to new worlds where you find better opportunities and greater possibilities than you ever knew before. When the average person meets disappointment he usually declares,

"Just my luck;" in other words, he enters that mental attitude that faces ill luck; he thus fails to see anything else but misfortune in that which has happened; and so long as that person, consciously or unconsciously expects misfortune, into more and more misfortune he will go. He who believes that he is fated to have bad luck will have bad luck in abundance. The reason is he lives in that mental attitude that places his mind in constant contact with those confused elements in the world that never create anything else but bad luck. That person, however, who thoroughly believes that everything that happens is simply a step to greater good, higher attainments and greater achievements, will steadily rise into those greater things that he expects to realize; the reason being that he is living in that mental attitude that places his mind in contact with the building power of life. Those powers will always build for greater things to those with whom they are in harmony, and we all can place ourselves in harmony with those powers; therefore, we can all move upward and onward forever, eternally making real more and more of that which is ideal.

What we expect comes if our expectation is filled with all the power of life and soul, and what we believe our fate to be, that is the kind of a fate we will create for ourselves. To meet ill luck in the belief that it is your luck, your particular kind of luck, and that it is natural for you to have that kind of luck is to stamp your own mind as an unlucky mind. This will produce chaotic thinking, which will cause you to do everything at the wrong time, and all your energies will be more or less misdirected; in consequence, bad luck and misfortune must necessarily follow. Bad luck comes from doing the wrong thing, or from being your worst; while good luck comes from being your best and from doing the right thing at the right time. It is therefore mere simplicity to create good luck at any time and in the measure that we may desire. The person that fears misfortune or expects misfortune and faces life in that attitude is concentrating attention upon misfortune; he thereby creates a world of misfortune in his own mind; and he who lives in mental misfortune will produce misfortune in his external life. Like causes produce like effects; and this explains why the things we fear always come upon us. We create mental causes for those things, and corresponding tangible effects always follow. Train the mind to expect the right and the best, regardless of present circumstances, conditions or events. Call everything good that is met. Declare that everything that happens, happens for the best. Meet everything in that frame of mind, and no matter how wrong or adverse conditions seem to be, you cause them all to work out right.

When the mind expects the best, has the faith that the right will prevail, and constantly faces the superior, the true mental attitude has been gained. Through that attitude all the forces of mind and all the powers of will become constructive, and will build for man the very thing that he expects or desires while his mind is fixed upon the ideal. He relates himself harmoniously to the best that is in all things and thus unites the ideal with the real in all things; and when the ideal becomes one with the real, the ideal desired becomes an actual fact in the real; and this is the goal every true idealist has in view. He takes those elements that have been revealed to him through the vision of the soul and blends them harmoniously with the actions of daily life. He thus brings the ideal down to earth and causes the real of every day life to express the ideal in everything that he may undertake to do. His life, his thought, his action, his attainments, his achievements, all contain that happy state where the ideal and the real are made one. His dreams have become true. The visions of the soul are actually realized, and the tangible is animated with that ideal something that makes personal existence all that any one could wish it to be.

First Step Towards Complete Emancipation

To forgive everybody for everything at all times, regardless of circumstances, is the first step towards complete emancipation. Heretofore, we have looked upon forgiveness as a virtue; now we know it to be a necessity. To those who possessed the spirit of forgiveness we have given our highest praise, and have thought of such people as being self sacrificing in the truest sense of that term. We did not know that the act of forgiving is the simplest way to lighten one's own burdens. According to our former conception of this subject, the man who forgives denies himself a privilege, the privilege of indignation and revenge; for this reason we have looked upon him as a hero or as a saint, thinking that it could not be otherwise than heroic and saintly to give up the supposed pleasure of meting out revenge to those who seemed to deserve it. According to the new view, however, the man who forgives is no more saintly than the one who insists upon keeping clean, because in reality the act of forgiving simply constitutes a complete mental bath. When you forgive everybody for everything you cleanse your mind completely of every wrong thought or adverse mental attitude that may exist in your consciousness. This explains why forgiveness is a necessity and why the man who forgives everything emancipates himself from all kinds of burdens. It is therefore profitable, most highly profitable, to forgive everybody, no matter what they have done, and this includes also ourselves. It is just as necessary to forgive ourselves as to forgive others, and the principal reason why forgiveness has seemed to be so difficult is because we have neglected to forgive ourselves.

We cannot let go of that which is not desired until we have acquired the mental art of letting go, and to acquire this art we must practice upon our own minds. That is, we must learn to let go from our own minds all those things that we do not wish to retain. When you forgive yourself completely you wash your mentality perfectly clean. You let go of everything in your mental system that is not good. You emancipate yourself completely. Whatever you held against yourself or others you now drop entirely out of your mind; in consequence, you are freed from your mental burdens, and when mental burdens disappear all other burdens will disappear also. The ills that we hold in mind are the only things that can actually burden our lives. Therefore, when we forgive everybody for every ill we ever knew we no longer hold a single ill in our own minds; we thus throw off every burden and are perfectly free. This also includes disease, because disease is nothing but a temporary effect of a wrong that we mentally hold in the system. Forgive everybody, including yourself, for everything, and all disease will vanish from your system. This may at first sight appear to be a startling statement, but it is the truth, and anyone can prove it to be the truth. "As a man thinketh in his heart so is he." Therefore, when every wrong is eliminated from the heart of man there can be no wrong in the man himself, and every wrong is eliminated from that heart that forgives everything in everyone. Many persons, however, will state that they hold no ill against anyone yet suffer just the same. So they may think, nevertheless they are mistaken and will see their mistakes when they learn the truth about mental laws. You may not hold direct ill against any person just now, but your mind has not always been absolutely pure and absolutely free from every wrong thought. You have had many wrong desires in your heart, and have had many mistaken ideas. To hold a mistaken idea is to hold a wrong in your heart. To have wrong desires is to hold ills against yourself, as well as others. To blame yourself, criticize yourself, feel provoked at yourself or condemn yourself for your shortcomings is to hold ills against yourself, and there are very few who are not doing this every day to some degree.

When we forgive all and still suffer we may not believe that forgiveness produces emancipation; but the fact is that suffering is impossible when forgiveness is absolute. When we forgive completely we shall also eliminate completely every trouble or ill that may exist in our world. When you have trouble forgive those who have caused the trouble; forgive yourself for permitting yourself to be troubled, and your troubles will pass away. When you have made a mistake do not condemn yourself or feel upset; simply forgive yourself, and resolve that you will never make the mistake again. As you make that resolution, desire more wisdom, and have the faith that you will secure the wisdom you require. "According to your faith so shall it be." There are many who will think that the practice of forgiving everybody for everything will produce mental indifference and thus weaken character, but it is the very opposite that will take place. To forgive is to eliminate the useless, everything that is not good; and to free the mind from obstacles and adverse conditions is to enable that mind to be its best, to express itself fully and completely. This will not only strengthen the character and enlarge the mind, but will cause the greatness of the soul to come forth. There is many a character that appears to be strong on account of its open hostility to wrongs, but such a character is not always strong. Too often it is composed of a few borrowed ideas about morality backed up by mere animal force.

The true character does not express hostility and does not resist or antagonize, but overcomes evil by giving all its power to the building of the good. A strong character meets evil with a silent indifference; that is, indifference in appearance only. The true character does not pass evil by because he does not care, but because he does care. He cares so much that he will not waste one single moment in prolonging the life of the wrong; therefore gives his whole time and attention to the making of good so strong that evil becomes absolutely powerless in the presence of that good. No intelligent person would antagonize darkness. By giving his time to the production of light he causes the darkness to disappear of itself.

When we apply the same principle to the elimination of evil a marvelous change for the better will come over the world. No person can forgive everybody for everything until he desires the best from every person and from every source. In other words, we cannot forgive the wrong until we desire the right. Therefore, the letting go of the inferior and the appropriation of the superior constitutes one and the same single mental process. We cannot eliminate darkness until we proceed to produce light, and it requires only the one act for removing the one and bringing forth the other. From these facts it is evident that when we let go of the wrong we gain more of that power that is right, and we thus increase the strength of character. To eliminate diseased conditions from the body will increase the strength of the body and will place the body in a position for further development, if we desire to promote such development. Likewise, to eliminate all ill feelings, all hatred, all wrong thoughts and all false beliefs from the mind will increase the power of the mind and place every mental faculty in proper condition for higher development. The same effect will be produced in the character, and all awakened minds know that the greatness of the soul can begin to come forth only when we have completely forgiven everybody for everything.

The man who finds it easier to forgive than to condemn is on the verge of superior wisdom and higher spiritual power. He has entered the path to real greatness and may rapidly rise in the scale by applying the laws of true human development. Instead of producing weakness and indifference the act of absolute forgiveness will produce a more powerful character, a more brilliant mind and a greater soul. Try this method for a year. Forgive everybody for everything, no matter what happens, and do not forget to forgive yourself. You will then conclude that forgiveness, absolute forgiveness, is not only the path to complete emancipation, but is also the "gates ajar" to a better life, a larger life, a richer life, a more beautiful life than you ever knew before. You will find that you can instantaneously remove disease from the body, perversion and wrong from the mind by complete and unrestricted forgiveness; and you can in the same way steadily recreate yourself into a new and better being. Forgive the imperfect, and with heart and soul desire constantly the realization of the perfect; the imperfect will thus pass away and the more perfect will be realized in a greater and greater abundance.

Whatever our place in life may be, we must eliminate every burden of mind or body, if we wish to rise in the scale, and the first step in this direction is to forgive everybody for everything. When you begin to practice forgiveness on this extensive scale you will find obstacles disappearing one after the other. Those things that held you down will vanish and that which was constantly in your way will trouble you no more; your pathway will be cleared. You will have nothing more to contend with, and everything in your life will move smoothly and harmoniously towards greater and greater things. This is perfectly natural, because by forgiving everybody and everything you have let every form of evil go. You have invited all the good, and have therefore populated your own world with persons and things after your own heart. Through perpetual and complete forgiveness your mind will be kept perfectly clean. Not a single weed will ever appear in the beautiful garden of your mind, and so long as the mind is clean neither sickness nor adversity can exist in human life. This may be a strong statement, but those who will try the principle and continue to live it will find it to be the truth.

Since forgiveness is a necessity to all who wish to eliminate the lesser and retain the greater, or in other words make real the ideal, it will be highly important to present the simplest methods through which anyone may learn to practice this great art. It has been said that to know all is to forgive all; but it is not possible for anyone to know all. Therefore, if we wish to forgive absolutely, we must proceed along a different line. When we ask ourselves why people live, think and act as they do we meet the great law of cause and effect. In our study of this law we find that every cause is an effect of a previous cause, and that that previous cause is also an effect of a cause still more remote. We may continue to trace these causes and effects far back along the chain of events until we are lost in the dimness of the past; but what do we learn by such a process of analysis, nothing whatever. We fail to find anything definite about anybody, and consequently cannot fix the blame for anything; but it is not possible to justly blame anybody when we cannot fix the blame for anything. Therefore, we have only one alternative, and that is to forgive. We can never find the real cause of a single thing. We may first blame the individual, but when we discover the influence of environment, heredity and early training we cannot wholly blame the individual. If we blame the parents, we must find the reason why those parents were not different, also why previous generations were not different. If we accept the theory that the individual has lived before and that he came into his present environments because he was what he was in a previous state of existence, we must explain why be did not live a different life in that other existence; why did he act in such a manner in the past that he should merit adversity and weakness in the present. If he knew no better in the past., what is the reason that he did not know any better? If we accept the belief that we have all inherited our perverted tendencies from Adam and Eve, we must explain why those two souls were not strong enough to rise above temptation. If they were tempted, we must explain why; we must explain why the original man who was created in the image and likeness of God did not express his divine nature in the midst of temptation. But there is no way in which we can explain these things; therefore, to fix the blame for anything is absolutely impossible.

The more we try to find the original cause of anything the more convinced we become that to look for sin or the cause of sin is nothing but a waste of time. Every individual is himself a cause, and his life comes constantly in touch with a number of other causes; therefore, it is never possible to say which one of these causes or combination of these causes produced the original action. Back of every action we find other actions that lead us to the one that we may now consider, but we do not know how those other actions were produced. To trace them back to their original source simply leads us into what appears to be a beginningless beginning. For this reason it is the height of wisdom to let the "dead bury its dead," to let the past go, to forgive every sinner and forget every sin, and to use our time, talent and power for the building of more lofty mansions in the great eternal now. To look for the blame is to find that we are all more or less to blame, and also to find that there is no real fixed blame anywhere. We may then ask what we are to do with this great subject; are we to talk, theorize, speculate, condemn and punish? We know too well that all of that is but a waste of time. The sensible course to pursue is to forgive everybody for everything, to drop ills, mistakes, wrongs, disagreeable memories and proceed to use those laws of life that we understand now in making life better for everybody now.

The man who is habitually doing wrong is mentally or morally sick. Punishment is a waste of time; besides, it is absolutely wrong, and one wrong cannot remove another. Such a person should be taken where he can be healed and kept there until he is well. We should not hate him or condemn him any more than those who are physically sick. Sickness is sickness whether it appears in the body, the mind or the character, and he who is sick does not need a prison; he needs a physician. To absolutely remove this hatred for the wrongdoers in the world we must cultivate a higher order of love, that love that loves every living creature with the true love of the soul, and such a love is readily attained when we train ourselves to look for the ideal soul of life that exists in everything everywhere in the world. This idea may cause many to come to the conclusion that the act of forgiving the wrongdoer will have an undesirable effect upon society, because we may be liable to let people in general do as they please; but in this they are wholly mistaken. Reason declares that you cannot justly blame anyone, and love does not wish to blame anyone; forgiveness must therefore inevitably follow when reason and love are truly combined; but reason and love will never permit man in general to do as he pleases. When we love people we are not indifferent about their future: We do not wish them to go down grade. We want them to improve, to do the right and the best and we will do everything in our power to emancipate and elevate the entire race. Reason understands how the laws of life can be applied in producing those results we may have in view; therefore, the desires of love can be carried out through the understanding of reason, and thus every high purpose may be promoted by the right spirit and the proper methods. Others may declare that these methods are in advance of our time and cannot be carried out at present; therefore, it is useless to even talk about it. However, be that as it may, the fact remains that forgiveness is a necessity to the true life, the emancipated life, the superior life, the ideal life. For that reason every person who desires to make real the ideal in his world must begin to practice absolute forgiveness at once. If we can forgive everybody for everything now, we should do so, whether the world in general can do so or not. The man who wishes to move forward must not wait for the race. It is his privilege to go in advance of the race; thus he prepares the way for millions.

When he has demonstrated by example that there are better ways of living, the race will follow. What the few can do today the many will do tomorrow, but if the few should wait until tomorrow, the many would have to wait until the day following, or possibly longer still. Be what you can be now. Do what you can do now, no matter how far in advance of this age such actions may be. If you are capable of greater things today, you owe it to the race to demonstrate those greater things now. You sprung from the race. You are composed of the finer elements that exist in the race, and should consider it a privilege to cause those elements to shine as brilliantly as possible; and one of the greatest of all demonstrations in this age is that of absolute forgiveness, to demonstrate the power of forgiving everybody for everything at all times and under every possible circumstance. We therefore conclude that complete emancipation from everything that is not desired in life can be realized only when we forgive absolutely in this great universal sense; and when we have forgiven everybody for everything, then we can say with the great Master Mind, "My yoke is easy and my burden is light."

Paths to Perpetual Increase

The universe is overflowing with all manner of good things and there is enough to supply every wish of every heart with abundance still remaining. How every heart is to proceed, however, that its every wish may be supplied, has been the problem, but the solution is simple. In consequence, everybody may rejoice. This world is not a "vale of tears," but is in truth a most delightful place, and is endowed with everything that is needful to make the life of man an endless song. We now know that we do not live to be miserable, but to rejoice. The bitterness that sometimes appears in life is not a real part of life. The greatness of existence alone is intended for man. To know the bitter from the sweet and to appropriate the latter and always reject the former is a matter, however, that is not clearly understood. There may be thousands who know the bitter when they see it, but they do not always know how to reject it. To throw off the ills of life is an art that few have mastered. But those who can eliminate the wrong are not always able to distinguish the right from the wrong, the reason being that we have not looked at things from the viewpoint of that power that produces things. The philosophers, the theologians and the scientists, as a rule, make life very complex and difficult to live. Their profound expressions confuse the multitudes, while ills and troubles continue as before; but to live is simple. Even a child can be happy; it therefore should not be difficult for anyone else.

When we realize happiness in its highest, broadest sense, we find that it comes in its fullness only when we have everything that the heart desires; and since the desires of the heart increase in size and number with the enlargement of life, the joy of living will increase in proportion providing all the, desires of the heart are supplied. This fact, however, may at first sight seem to make happiness very difficult to secure. If we cannot enjoy the allness of joy until we have everything that heart can wish for, then happiness is far away; so it may seem, but things are not always what they seem. All things are possible, and the most difficult. Things become comparatively easy when we know how; therefore, the way of wisdom is not to look for those difficulties that ignorance has connected with things, but look for that simplicity that is the soul of all knowledge. When we learn to do things as they should be done, all difficulties disappear, and even the largest life becomes simple.

The doing of things is the universal theme in this age. Those who simply tell us what to do are no longer acceptable. We want practical instructions that tell us how. The greatest man of this age and of the future will not be the one who can move as he wishes the emotions of multitudes by the magic art of eloquence and bring whole nations to his feet by the artistic juggling of eloquent phrases. The great man will henceforth be the man who can tell us how, and who can express himself so clearly that anyone can understand. This, however, we are now beginning to do, and ere long the many will come back to the truth itself and understand the real truth in all its original simplicity. The path of truth and life is perfectly straight and is illumined all the way. It is therefore simplicity itself to follow this path when we find it, but the many have strayed into the jungles of illusions and misconceptions. These must all come back to the simple path, and when they do the difficulty of living will wholly disappear.

To teach the race how to find the simple things, the true things and the real things is now the purpose of every original thinker, and whoever can add to the world's wisdom in this respect becomes a light to the race, indeed. One of the first principles in this new understanding of things is that which deals with man's power to place himself in perfect touch with the source of limitless supply; in other words to enter the path of perpetual increase. As previously stated, the world is overflowing with good things, because life is in touch with the limitless source of all good things, and there is so much of everything that the wish of every heart can be gratified. We do not have to take from another to have abundance, because there is more than sufficient for all. The fact that some one has abundance does not prove that he has taken some or all of his wealth from others, although this is what a great many believe to be the truth. Whenever we see some one in luxury we wonder where and how he got it, and we usually add that many are in poverty because this one is in wealth. Such doctrine, however, is not true. It is thoroughly false from beginning to end. The world is not so poverty stricken that the few cannot have plenty without stealing from the many. The universe is not so bare and so limited that multitudes are reduced to want whenever a few persons undertake to surround themselves with those things that have beauty and worth. True, there is injustice in the world. There are people who have secured their wealth, not upon merit, but through the art of reducing others to want; but the remedy is not to be found in the doctrine that thousands must necessarily become poor when one becomes very rich. This doctrine is an illusion, and illusions cannot serve as foundations for a better order. There is enough in life to give every living person all the wealth and all the luxury that he can possibly appropriate.

God is rich; the universe is overflowing with abundance. If we have not everything that we want, there is a reason; there is some definite cause somewhere, either in ourselves or in our relations to the world, but this cause can be found and corrected; then we may proceed to take possession of our own. Among the many causes of poverty and the lack of a full supply there is one that has been entirely overlooked. To overcome this cause is to find one of the most important paths to perpetual increase, and the remedy lies within easy reach of everyone who has awakened to a degree the finer elements in his life.

There may be exceptions to the rule, but there are thousands who are living on the husks of existence because they were not grateful when the kernels were received. Multitudes continue in poverty from no other cause than a lack of gratitude, and other thousands who have almost everything that the heart may wish for do not reach the coveted goal of full supply because their gratitude is not complete.

We are now beginning to realize more and more that the greatest thing in the world is to live so closely to the Infinite that we constantly feel the power and the peace of His presence. In fact, this mode of living is the very secret of secrets revealing everything that the mind may wish to know or understand in order to make life what it is intended to be. We also realize that the more closely we live to the Infinite the more we shall receive of all good things, because all good things have their source in the Supreme; but how to enter into this life of supreme oneness with the Most High is a problem. There are many things to be done in order to solve this problem, but there is no one thing that is more important in producing the required solution than deep, whole souled gratitude. The soul that is always grateful lives nearer the true, the good, the beautiful and the perfect than anyone else in existence, and the more closely we live to the good and the beautiful the more we shall receive of all those things. The mind that dwells constantly in the presence of true worth is daily adding to his own worth. He is gradually and steadily appropriating that worth with which he is in constant contact; but we cannot enter into the real presence of true worth unless we fully appreciate the real worth of true worth; and all appreciation is based upon gratitude.

The more grateful we are for the good things that come to us now the more good things we shall receive in the future. This is a great metaphysical law, and we shall find it most profitable to comply exactly with this law, no matter what the circumstances may be. Be grateful for everything and you will constantly receive more of everything; thus the simple act of being grateful becomes a path to perpetual increase. The reason why is found in the fact that whenever you enter into the mental attitude of real gratitude your mind is drawn into much closer contact with that power that produces the good things received. In other words, to be grateful for what we have received is to draw more closely to the source of that which we receive. The good things that come to us come because we have properly employed certain laws, and when we are grateful for the results gained we enter into more perfect harmony with those laws and thus become able to employ those laws to still greater advantage in the immediate future. This anyone can understand, and those who do not know that gratitude produces this effect should try it and watch results.

The attitude of gratitude brings the whole mind into more perfect and more harmonious relations with all the laws and powers of life. The grateful mind gains a firmer hold, so to speak, upon those things in life that can produce increase. This is simply illustrated in personal experience where we find that we always feel nearer to that person to whom we express real gratitude. When you thank a person and truly mean it with heart and soul you feel nearer to that person than you ever did before. Likewise, when we express whole souled thanksgiving to everything and everybody for everything that comes into life we draw closer and closer to all the elements and powers of life. In other words, we draw closer to the real source from which all good things in life proceed.

When we consider this principle from another point of view we find that the act of being grateful is an absolute necessity, if we wish to accomplish as much as we have the power to accomplish. To be grateful in this large, universal sense is to enter into harmony and contact with the greatest, the highest and the best in life. We thus gain possession of the superior elements of mind and soul and, in consequence, gain the power to become more and achieve more, no matter what our object or work may be. Everything that will place us in a more perfect relation with life, and thus enable us to appropriate the greater richness of life, should be employed with the greatest of earnestness, and deep whole souled gratitude does possess a marvelous power in this respect. Its great value, however, is not confined to the laws just mentioned. Its power is exceptional in another and equally important field.

To be grateful is to think of the best, therefore the grateful mind keeps the eye constantly upon the best; and, according to another metaphysical law, we grow into the likeness of that which we think of the most. The mind that is always dissatisfied fixes attention upon the common, the ordinary and the inferior, and thus grows into the likeness of those things. The creative forces within us are constantly making us just like those things upon which we habitually concentrate attention. Therefore, to mentally dwell upon the inferior is to become inferior, while to keep the eye single upon the best is to daily become better. The grateful mind is constantly looking for the best, thus holding attention upon the best and daily growing into the likeness of the best. The grateful mind expects only good things, and will always secure good things out of everything that comes. What we constantly expect we receive, and when we constantly expect to get good out of everything we cause everything to produce good. Therefore, to the grateful mind all things will at all times work together for good, and this means perpetual increase in everything that can add to the happiness and the welfare of man. This being true, and anyone can prove it to be true, the proper course to pursue is to cultivate the habit of being grateful for everything that comes. Give thanks eternally to the Most High for everything and feel deeply grateful every moment to every living creature. All things are so situated that they can be of some service to us, and all things have somewhere at sometime been instrumental in adding to our welfare. We must therefore, to be just and true, express perpetual gratitude to everything that has existence. Be thankful to yourself. Be thankful to every soul in the world, and most of all be thankful to the Creator of all that is. Live in perpetual thanksgiving to all the world, and express the deepest, sincerest, most whole souled gratitude you can feel within whenever something of value comes into your life.

When other things come, pass them by; never mind them in the least. You know that the good in greater and greater abundance is eternally coming into your life, and for this give thanks with rejoicing; you know that every wish of the heart is being supplied; be thankful that this is true, and you will draw nearer and nearer to that place in life where that can be realized that you know is on the way to realization. Live according to this principle for a brief period of time, and the result will be that your life will change for the better to such a degree that you will feel infinitely more grateful than you ever felt before. You will then find that thanksgiving is a necessary part of real living, and you will also find that the more grateful you are for every ideal that has been made real, the more power you gain to press on to those greater heights where you will find every ideal to be real. And when this realization begins you are on the path to perpetual increase, because the more you receive the more grateful you feel, and the more grateful you feel for that which has been received the more closely you will live to that Source that can give you more.

Consider The Lilies

Consider the lilies of the field, how they grow; they toil not, neither do they spin; yet I say unto you, that even Solomon in all his glory was not arrayed like one of these. Matt. 6; 28, 29.

The greatest service that anyone can render to the race is to properly fill the place he occupies now, to be himself today; but it is not only others that will benefit by such individual actions. The individual himself will receive greater good from life through this method than through all other methods combined. The great secret of secrets is to live your own life in your own world as well as you possibly can now. In this age thousands are seeking the path of spiritual growth and high intellectual attainments, while millions are dreaming of the life beautiful; accordingly, systems almost without number are springing up everywhere, claiming to reveal the hidden path to these greater goals; but it is the truth that when everything has been said, the one statement that rises above them all is this: Be all that you are today and you shall be even more tomorrow. If you are in search of higher spiritual and intellectual attainments enter into every form of wisdom that surrounds you today and fill your life with as much spirit as you can possibly realize. If you wish to live an ideal life, then aim to make real the most beautiful life that you can think of today. If you are longing for greater accomplishments and a larger sphere of usefulness, then be your very best in the place that you occupy now.

The mighty oak grows great because it grows in the present; it does not think of the past or the future; it is what it is now; it does not wish to become mighty; it simply grows on silently and continually. The lily of the field is beautiful because it is perfectly satisfied to be a lily, but it is not satisfied to be less than all a lily can be. It does not strive or work hard to become beautiful; it simply goes on being what it is, and the result is it has been made immortal by the greatest mind that ever lived. When we follow the example of the lily we find the real secret of life, so simply and clearly stated that any one can understand. Be what you are today. Do not be satisfied to be less than you can today and do not strive to be more. Progress, growth, advancement, attainment, these do not come through overreaching. The mind that overreaches will have a reaction; he will fall to the bottom and will have to begin all over again. Real attainment comes by being your best where you are just for today, by filling the present moment with all the life you are conscious of; no more. If you try to express more life than you can comfortably feel in consciousness, you are overreaching and you will have a fall. The great mistake of the age is to strive, to go about our work as if it were extremely difficult. The man who works the hardest usually accomplishes the least; while the truly great man is the man who has trained his life and his power to work through him.

The lilies of the field are not engaged in hard labor, and yet their usefulness cannot be measured; they are fulfilling their true purpose; they are making real the ideal in their own world and they are living inspirations to every soul in existence. They live to be beautiful and they become beautiful, not by being ambitious for beauty, but by permitting all the beauty they possess to come forth. What is within us is constantly pressing for expression. We do not have to call it forth nor labor so much to bring it into action. All we are required to do is to permit ourselves to be what we are, to permit what is within to express itself fully and completely. We do not have to work so hard to become great. We are all naturally great, and our potential greatness is ever ready to manifest, if we would only cease our striving and let life live. The lily is beautiful because it does not hinder its own inherent beauty from coming forth to be seen; but if the lily should take up the strenuous life it would in one generation become a despised weed. The human race today resembles in too many instances the useless weed. Millions in every generation come and go without accomplishing anything whatever. They do not even live a life that gives contentment. The reason is they strive too much, and in their striving destroy the very powers that can produce greatness. We have worked hard for results, not knowing that the only cause of results was within us, ready to produce the very results we desired, just for the asking. We have in many instances destroyed our brains trying to invent methods for producing health, happiness, power and success, not knowing that these things already existed within us in abundant supply, and that by wholesome thinking they would appear in full external expression.

The secret of secrets is to let the best within us have full right of way; this, however, most of us have failed to do. In consequence, the majority are undeveloped weaklings of little use to themselves or to the world. The lily permits that which is to have right of way. It does not interfere, but man does interfere. He usually refuses to accept the gifts which nature wishes to bestow upon him, and he hardly ever accepts assistance from a higher power. He sets out for himself and works himself into old age and death trying to gain what was actually given to him in the beginning. He leaves the real riches of life and enters the world of personal ambition expecting to find something better and create something superior through his own efforts, but he fails because man alone can do nothing. The average person does not realize that to create something from nothing is impossible, nor has he learned that the necessary something can come only from the life that is within. He may try to accomplish much and become much through personal ambition and hard work, but no one can build without material, and the material that is needed in building greatness can be secured only by giving right of way to the life and the power of the inner world. The man who expects to build greatness upon personal limitations will pass away in the effort, leaving his unfinished work to be taken up by some one else who will possibly build upon the same useless foundation. Thus one generation after another comes and goes, each expecting to succeed where predecessors failed; in the meantime very little is accomplished by man, and he fails to receive what infinite life is ever waiting to give.

This is the truth about man in general. The multitudes have come and gone during countless ages and have accomplished but little. There have been a few great exceptions in every age, but these were exceptions because they refused to follow the ways of the world. They learned the lesson that the lilies have taught, and they chose to let life live, to let the greatness from within come forth, to let power work, and to let that which is in the real of man have full right of way. When a person discovers what he is and permits that which he is to have full expression, his days of weariness, trouble and failure are gone. Henceforth he will live as the flower. His life will be full. He will fulfill his purpose and eternally become more and more of that which already is in the great within. When a flower, which has so little of soul within itself, can become so much by permitting itself to be itself, how much more might man become if he would permit himself to be himself. Man is created in the image of God, therefore marvels are hidden within his wonderful soul. When these marvels are given full expression then man begins to become that which the Infinite intended that he should be. In the soul of the lily is hidden the spirit of beauty; nothing more. But the lily does not hinder this spirit from appearing in visible form; therefore, it becomes an inspiration of joy to all the world. In the soul of man even the Infinite is hidden; we can therefore imagine what man will become when he permits the spirit of divinity to express itself in his personal form. This is a great truth, indeed, and deserves constant attention from every mind that has learned to think.

We may believe that every step forward that we have taken has been produced through personal efforts and hard work, but in this we are mistaken.

In the first place, those achievements that have followed hard work are always insignificant and never of any permanent value, but those steps forward that have permanent value and that are truly great we find were taken during those moments when we permitted real life to live. We therefore find that striving accomplishes nothing, while we may through living, accomplish anything. There are times when many of us cease our strenuous labor for a few moments and unconsciously open our souls to that higher something that we feel so much the need of when wearied with misdirected labors, and the influx of real life that comes at such times is the cause of those real steps upward and onward that we have taken. At such times we chose to be like the lily; we permitted the good that was to come forth; we gave up, so to speak, to higher power and did not interfere with its highest, fullest expression. What we gain at such moments is always with us and never fails to give us strength, power and inspiration even when we decide for the time being to adopt the ways of the world once more. But since every step in advance comes when we refuse to go the way of the world, we should now understand that the way of the world is a mistake. We should therefore free ourselves from that mode of life, thought and action absolutely.

The world seeks to gain greater things through personal ambition and hard work. The true way to attain greater things is to permit the greatness that is within to have full expression; likewise when we seek health, happiness and harmony or a beautiful life, the true course is to permit those things to come forth and act through us; they are ready to appear. We do not have to work for them or strive so hard to secure them. They are now at hand and will express themselves through us the very moment we grant them permission. We have all discovered that whenever we become perfectly still and permit supreme life to live in us we can feel power accumulating in our system until we feel as if we could move mountains. We have also felt that while turning attention to the everlasting joy within and opening the mind fully to this joy that there came into being a state of happiness, comfort and contentment that seemed infinitely more perfect than the imagination has ever pictured the joys of heaven to be. Likewise when we failed to find health in the without or through external means we invariably found the precious gift coming from within, the moment we gave up, so to speak, to its wholesome life and power.

In this age personal ambition is one of the ruling factors, and nearly everybody is trying to outdo some one else. The result is we build up and tear down in the outer world, but as a race we improve but little. The great within is ignored, held back or prevented from free expression, while there are few things in the great without that are really worth while. There never was a time when we should consider the lilies of the field more than now. The human race is breaking itself down striving to gain hold upon phantoms, while the great prize that has already been given is lost sight of in the dust and confusion. But to inspire the present generation with a desire to return to nature and her beautiful ways cannot be done to any extent, however, except through living examples. It is the living of life that will change the life of the world. The world at large does not listen to reason, nor can those who are in the mad rush stop to think; besides, such minds are not sufficiently clear to understand the principles upon which the living of life is based. Seeing is believing, as far as the world is concerned, and therefore they require living examples of those who have proven the superiority of the better way; accordingly, those who know how to live as the lilies live should consider it a privilege to place their light wherever it can be seen. When you can prove through your own life and experience that personal ambition and hard work are not necessary to greater things, but are actual hindrances, and that greater things come of themselves to those who will permit themselves to be themselves, you have caused a great light to spring up, and few there are who will not see it. Those who take everything literally may wonder how anything can be accomplished without work, but they must bear in mind that there is work, and work. The work that is done by those who are down in the world's way is hard, wearing and tearing. It is destructive to human life and builds up one thing by tearing down another, and in the end it brings no lasting good, neither to the individual nor to the race; but the work that is done by those who have found the better way is neither hard nor wearisome. It is not done through strenuous living nor external striving, but is done by the power of the great within coming forth into expression in personal life. In this mode of work you first give your inner power right of way, then you direct it consciously and intelligently. You do not depend upon personal power and difficult personal efforts. You place yourself in the hands of higher power, and as you receive higher power you cause it to do that which you wish to have done. You have all felt power working through you, and at such times work was pleasure. You gave the commands, of course, and you knew it was your own power, your own higher power, but no hard personal effort was required. You simply opened the way somehow, then decided firmly but gently what you wished to have done; and you could feel a mighty power coming forth, seemingly from an inexhaustible source, taking full possession of thought and muscle, and doing the very thing you desired to have done. After the work was finished you discovered it was superior work, and although you had engaged in the task for many hours you actually felt stronger than when you began.

The reason why is simple. You did not depend upon personal limitations and strenuous efforts; and you did not try to make those limitations do a great deal more than they had the capacity to do. You opened your life to all the power of your life and you thus received enough power to do what you wished to have done, and more; and so long as you have power to spare you can be neither weak nor tired. When the system is thoroughly full of energy, work is a pleasure; and so long as that fullness continues weariness is impossible; and there is enough power in real life to cause your system to be full of energy, and more, at all times no matter how much you may do or how great your task may be.

When we consider the lilies of the field, how they grow, we find that they naturally permit the life that is within them to unfold; they do not try to grow; they have, as everything has, the power of growth within them and they grow because they do not hinder that interior power and growth from having their way. Likewise, when we know that divinity reigns within us we do not have to work hard nor many years to reach that state. We will grow and develop, both mentally and spiritually, when we permit the divinity within to unfold. Everything seeks self expression. Nothing in nature, visible or invisible, will have to be forced into expression, because at the very heart of all things there is the deep, strong desire to come forth and be. Therefore, if we wish to ascend in the scale of life, we must cease those confused and destructive states of mind that hinder expression, and become as the lilies of the field. Give the life within permission to really live in us. The life within will live our life and give us a beautiful life. The power within will do our work and do that work extremely well. The divinity within will make us Godlike in all things, and never cease to give us the things of the spirit so long as we permit those things to come forth and abide in personal existence.

What we are required to do that such things may come to pass is to live, think and act in the likeness of the Infinite. God is, and He permits Himself to be what He is. Man must do likewise, and all shall be well with him. Those who do not understand may think that the individuality of man might diminish, if he were to give himself up to the life and the power within, but such a conclusion will disappear when we realize that the power from within is our own. We are simply causing ourselves to become more and more of what we already are in reality. By giving free expression to our own higher, interior powers we naturally become more powerful, and by giving free expression to our own inherent divinity we naturally become more Godlike and more spiritual on every plane of being. The lilies of the field do not become inferior lilies by permitting the spirit of the beautiful to unfold from within their gentle lives. It is by this method that they become what they are, and they become so much that the glory of artificial man can never compare with theirs. It is the same with the human soul. The soul becomes great and beautiful by permitting its own greatness and loveliness to come forth unhindered and undisturbed.

Thousands of people are at present trying to develop higher powers. Many of these actually try to work hard in their efforts to gain the various gifts of mind and soul, and because they do not succeed to any great extent they frequently become discouraged and give up, wondering whether or not the real truth has been found. Others being ambitious to become great in the world try to employ spiritual laws in the furthering of their personal aims, but they find the reactions so disagreeable that the prize is not worth the labor. To fly to the top at once is the ruling passion among many and when they fail with whatever methods they may employ they conclude that what passes for truth is nothing but man made doctrines. The fact is, however, that the truth always appears to be the untruth when misdirected. To apply the principles of real truth in the furthering of any lofty aim we may have in mind, the first essential is to establish life in perfect touch with eternal life; the second essential is to positively determine what we expect to attain and become in actual personal living; and the third essential is to proceed in the attainment of health, happiness and harmony. Without health nothing of permanent value can be accomplished. Without happiness our talents will be as the flowers without sunshine, and without harmony most of the power we might receive would be thrown away.

To obtain health, happiness and harmony we need simply let life live. Real life already has these things, and when we let life live in us those things will be expressed through us. The next essential is to resolve that we will be fully contented simply to live. To shine in the world, to acquire fame or to do something wonderful that mankind may long remember us, that we will not think of. Many a person has worked hard for fame and died early, in obscurity. Fame in itself, however, is of no value. When you are neither happy nor well, fame cannot make your life worth while. If you are miserable, it will profit nothing if everybody may know your name. It is not the praise of man that we should seek, but the life of the Infinite. The praise of the world can give us nothing, but life from within can give us everything that the heart can wish for.

True fame comes to him who deserves it without his trying to get it, but those only can deserve the honor of the race who have always been their best, who have not neglected a single opportunity to be of service, and who have lived constantly for the one purpose of being an inspiration to every soul. We may look at this phase of the subject as we may, we can come to only one conclusion. He alone is great and deserving of honor who so lives that he always is all that God made him to be; and it is such a life that is lived by the lilies of the field. When man will be as true to his large world as the lilies are to their small world, mankind will become a race of gods indeed, and the Utopian dreams of the prophets will come true. This, however, the ordinary thinker may declare to be impossible, but nothing is impossible. If a flower can be true to itself in its world, man can be true to himself in his world.

Those who are accustomed to the worldly methods of thinking and working may feel that it is hardly possibly to apply these new ideas while associated with worldly minds, but we must remember that it is not where we work or at what we work, but how we work that determines what results are to be. To work so that you permit the boundless power within to work through you is the secret, and this will not only cause your work to be pleasant, but will also cause you to do better and better work every day. It is therefore the royal path to pleasantness today and greater things tomorrow. In the old way you are compelled to almost wear yourself out today in order that you might provide for tomorrow; but not so in the new. While you are providing for tomorrow you are not only enjoying life today, but you are, through the expression of greater and greater power from within, making yourself larger, stronger and greater today. In the development of talents you employ the same principle. You do not strive for greatness; you know that you are potentially great already, and by permitting this greatness to become alive in you, you will accomplish great things.

When you apply this principle in everything that you do, you will find your advancement to be steady and even rapid; you will move forward in all things, making the ideal real as you ascend in the scale. The very moment you find a new ideal you find that power within you that can make that ideal real; thus your advancement becomes continuous, your progress eternal. To live the life beautiful we simply let life live. We know that life itself is beautiful and when we permit that life that is beautiful to live in us, we will live consciously and personally the most beautiful life that we can picture in the ideal without making any personal effort to do so. When we begin to live, think and act according to these principles we feel that we are carried on and on by some mysterious presence that seems to be doing everything for us while giving us the pleasure and the glory. We soon learn, however, that this presence is ourself, our own larger, superior self created in the image of God; therefore, able to do everything that we may wish to have done; and it is a joy, indeed, to feel everything moving so smoothly and gently, so harmoniously and pleasantly, and at the same time producing such great results.

To engage in some extraordinary work becomes one of our greatest pleasures, because nothing is hard or difficult any more; obstacles disappear the very moment we enter their presence, and we realize inwardly that whatever we undertake to do will be accomplished. We no longer tremble when in the midst of events that require exceptional wisdom and power; we know that wisdom is ready to speak whatever may be necessary now, and that power is at hand to do whatever may be necessary to be done now. We are in touch with the greatness of the great within and may draw upon that great, inexhaustible source whatever we may need at any time. Fear takes flight, while faith becomes stronger, higher and more perfect; sorrow and despair are no more, because all things are working for the best. Even in the presence of death and loss we see more life and greater gain. We know that what passes away merely ascends that it may live more and be itself in a larger, higher measure than it ever was before. We know that whatever comes will bring the new and the more beautiful. It could not be otherwise, because having chosen to be all that we are, the all can never cease to come, and the more the all continues to come the more the all will continue to bring. We have laid aside the illusions of the world and adopted the ways of truth. We have beheld the beauties of nature and have opened our minds to the visions of the soul. These have given us the secret, and like the lilies of the field, we have learned to be still and live.

Count It All Joy

We meet something at almost every turn that we think ought to be different. If we have high ideals, we may not feel satisfied to permit those conditions to remain as they are; we may even complain or antagonize. On the other hand, if our ideals be low, we may feel wholly indifferent, but then we find that those things go from bad to worse. What we seek, however, is our present comfort on the one hand and the betterment of everything about us on the other hand, and we wish to know how this may be brought about in the midst of the confusion, the ignorance and the ills that we find in the world. When we are indifferent to the wrong it becomes worse; therefore, even for our own good we must do something with those adverse conditions that exist in the home, in society, or in the state. We must meet all those things and meet them properly, but the problem is, how?

To antagonize, criticize or condemn never helps matters in the least; besides, such states of mind are a detriment to one's own peace and health. The critical mind wears itself out while thinking about the wrong, but the wrong in the meantime goes on becoming worse. To feel disappointed because the universe does not move according to our fancy will not change the universe, but it will produce weakness in our own mind and body. That person who lives constantly in the world of despondency will soon lose all hold upon life; he consequently does nothing in the world but bring about the end of his own personal life. The usual way of dealing with the problems of life solves nothing. The ordinary way of meeting temptation gives the tempter greater power, while the person who tries to resist is usually entrapped in adversity and trouble. But St. Paul has told us what to do under all such circumstances. Count it all joy. That is the secret. Count it all joy no matter what may come, agreeing with all adversity at once, antagonizing nothing; condemning no one, leaving criticism alone. Never be disappointed or discouraged, and have nothing whatever to do with worry. Whatever comes, count it all joy. He who meets adversity in the attitude of peace, harmony and joy will turn enemies into friends and failures into greater good.

When things do not come your way, never mind. Continue to count everything joy, and everything will change in such a manner as to give you joy. If you are seeking the best, all things will work together in such a way as to give you the best, and your heart's desire shall be realized; possibly not today, but life is long; you can wait. That which is good is always good; it is always welcome whenever it comes. In the meantime you are living in harmony and joy, and that in itself is surely a great good. That person who lives constantly in gloom drives even the sunshine out of his own mind; the clouds of gloom are so heavy that he fails to see the brightness that is all about him. That person, however, who counts everything joy will change everything to brightness and thus receive joy from everything. When you fail to receive what you sought, never for a moment be disappointed. Count it all joy. In fact, be supremely happy; you have a reason so to be. When you fail to get what you seek it simply means that there is something still better in store for you; then why should you not count such an event great joy. This is always the case when your whole desire is to receive the best; and when you train yourself to count everything joy, your mind develops that desire that always desires the best.

When you seek only the best, the best only will come, and you must not feel disappointed when you are taken away from a hovel in order that you may enter a palace. When you meet enemies or adversaries do not resist them or enter into warfare; look for terms of agreement. Possibly they may seem to get the best of the bargain now, but you can afford to give them the terms they ask. The Infinite is your supply. When one door closes another opens, and if you depend upon the Supreme to open that other door, it will be a door opening into far greater and far better things than what you seemingly lost; besides, by being kind to your adversary you lifted yourself up. You are now a higher and a greater being. That means that you will now draw to yourself higher and better things; consequently, it was not the enemy that got the best terms; it was you.

Whatever you are called upon to do, do it and be happy. Count it all joy that you are given the opportunity to bring sunshine into dark places and develop your own latent power by doing what seemed difficult. You are equal to the occasion, if you think so; therefore you should consider it a privilege to prove it. The world is waiting for great souls, souls that are ready to do what others failed to accomplish. You can become one of these great souls by proving to yourself that you are equal to every occasion; and you will be equal to every occasion, if you count everything joy. When you are in the midst of temptations, rejoice with your whole heart. You have found a great opportunity to turn wrong into right, and to turn wrong into right is always a mark of greatness. Millions of people have died unhonored and unsung who might have arisen to greatness and become leaders and saviors in the world, if they would have demonstrated their superiority in the midst of temptation, tribulation and wrong. Look upon all temptations and troubles as opportunities to make wrong right, and be glad that such opportunities have been presented to you. Count it all joy; besides, the result will not only produce joy to yourself, but possibly to millions. He who changes wrong into right rises in the scale, and you can think of no greater good coming to you than this. He who remains below must be counted with the small and the ordinary. He who goes up higher shall gain everything that his heart may wish for. Therefore, whatever comes, or whatever you meet, or whatever you are called upon to do, proceed with peace and joy. Be glad that you have the opportunity to prove your own power, and thus elevate yourself thereby. Be supremely happy to know that you may change many things for the better through this attitude, and thus bless the lives of multitudes.

Train yourself to look at things according to this principle, and you will find that everything can produce joy. Everything can give cause for rejoicing; that is, providing everything is met in that attitude that counts everything joy. The same principle may be employed to great advantage in overcoming difficulties. When you are asked to do what seems to be very difficult, or when you are called upon to perform duties you do not like, never refuse. Count it all joy. To excuse yourself when such occasions appear is to lose most valuable opportunities.

Every person desires to make the most of himself, but to accomplish this all latent power must be awakened, and there is nothing that will bring forth our latent powers more thoroughly than the doing of what seems difficult. When you find yourself shrinking from certain tasks you have discovered a weak faculty within yourself. Refuse to let that faculty remain in such a condition. Go and do what you feared to do and let nothing hold you back. In this way the weak faculty will be made strong and your entire nature will pass through most valuable discipline and training. Nothing is really disagreeable unless we think so. That is, we may approach the disagreeable in such a way that it ceases to be disagreeable; and the secret is, count everything joy. You may enter darkness and gloom, but if you are living in a world of brightness and cheer, that darkness will not be darkness to you, nor will gloom enter your mind for a moment. You can remain in your own happy world, no matter what may happen, no matter what may take place in your immediate environment.

When you resolve to do certain things and proceed with a conviction that you will enjoy the work thoroughly, you will find real pleasure in that work; besides, you will do the work very well. Pleasure comes from within, and when the fountain of joy within is overflowing, it will give joy to everything that exists about us. To cause this fountain within to overflow at all times, count everything joy at all times. We should never look for weakness, but when we find it we should proceed at once to change it into strength. Whenever we meet difficulties, or whenever we are called upon to do what we dislike we have found a weakness. We may remove that weakness by doing with a will what the moment demands, and resolve to enjoy it. Never permit such occasions to pass by without being changed. The opportunity is too valuable. Whatever your present sphere of action may require of you, that you are able to do; and the present demand upon your life and your talents must be supplied by you if you would bring out the best that is in you, and make the great eternal now full and complete.

Tasks that seem difficult and demands that seem unreasonable are after all neither difficult nor unreasonable. They are simply golden opportunities for you to become what you never were before. They are but paths to greater achievements, sweeter joys and a larger life. Therefore, when you meet such occasions, count it all joy. When you fail to gain or realize in the present what you expected, do not feel disappointed. Make up your mind to be just as happy in those conditions that are, as you expect to be in those conditions that you are looking for. The feeling of disappointment is not produced by events. It is produced by your own attitude toward events. You can meet all events in such a frame of mind that you never feel disappointed in the least, and that frame of mind is the result of counting everything joy. When you know that eternity is long and that countless joys are in store for you, you will not feel sad now because one insignificant event has been postponed. And when you have full control of your mind you will have the power to produce just as much happiness in the absence of that event as in its presence, because events themselves cannot produce happiness.

The same is true of things. We do not gain joy from things, but from the way we think about things, and we can think as we choose at any time no matter what the circumstance may be. When the present demands happiness from something different than what you were looking for in the present, grasp the opportunity to prove that you are equal to this occasion. You thus develop latent ability. When you count everything joy you know that you can always produce joy. You know that whatever happens is best, because you have the power to cause it to become the best. The best always happens to those who seek only the best; therefore, whatever comes should be received as the best, and we must give it the opportunity to prove that it is better than anything that could have happened. You are not dependent upon events for happiness. Happiness does not come from what we do or where we go. Happiness comes from what we are now or what we create out of what is present now. Whether we be alone in a garret or in a gorgeous ball room the amount of happiness we are to receive in either place will depend entirely upon our own frame of mind. The frame of mind that you desire for the present moment you may have; if it does not come of itself, you can create it; you are the master.

When things do not come the way we like, we can like them the way they are coming. This is how we agree quickly with our adversaries; we thus-receive the enemy instead of fighting the enemy; and that which we receive in the true attitude of mind becomes our own. Count everything joy and every adversity will give up its power to you. That which is evil becomes good when we meet it in such a way that we draw out of it the best that it may contain, and we always attract the best from everything when we meet everything in the conviction that all things work together for good. When nothing comes to give us happiness in the external we can open the fount of everlasting joy in the great within. The heaven of the soul is ever ready to open its pearly gates, but we must look towards the soul if we would pass through those gates. We shall fail to see the fountain of joy within, however, so long as our whole attention is fixed upon those worldly pleasures that failed to come into our world; but if we count everything joy we no longer feel disappointed about what did not happen; on the other hand we enter into that joyous state of mind that will place us in direct contact with the source of limitless joy within the mind. When people speak unkindly of you, you will become offended if you thought they spoke unkindly, but if your eyes are too pure to behold iniquity you will go on your way as if nothing had been said; you count everything joy and thus you will receive joy from your own lofty position in the matter.

When you are asked to do certain things do not proceed with a feeling that you are compelled to. Go and do it because you want to; say that you want to, and count it all joy. We should never say "I have a duty to perform," but rather, "Here is an opportunity which I have the privilege to embrace." Train yourself to want to do whatever your present sphere of life may demand. He who loves and thoroughly enjoys what he is doing today will be asked to do greater things tomorrow. The large soul never asks if things are unpleasant or difficult; such thoughts never enter his mind. Whatever he finds to do he proceeds to do, with his mind full of will and his heart full of joy. If you dislike anybody, you have found a weakness in yourself. You have found a difficulty that must be overcome at once. Do not permit such obstacles to remain in your way. The soul that knows no weakness loves everything that God has created. The strong soul never considers those imperfections in life that man has created. Intelligence was not intended to be used in the study of nothingness, illusions or mistakes. When we hate anything we recognize the existence and the power of those things that have neither real existence nor real power; we therefore enter into a confused state of mind. What God has created we cannot help but love, but if we see something else and dislike that something else we are seeing something that God has not created. In other words, we are giving attention to illusions and mistakes, and the mind is not intended for that purpose. Remove the illusion by transforming that hate into love; this will change the point of view. You will thus see things from the upper side, the divine side, and when we look at things from the divine side we find that everything is altogether lovely.

Therefore, when you dislike anybody overcome that weakness by giving that person all the love of your heart. Love that person and mean it, no matter what he has said or done. There is nothing in the world that lifts the soul so high above darkness and illusion as strong, pure, spiritual love; and it is not difficult to love a person when you know that he is God's creation, while his mistakes are simply man's creation. Mistakes must be forgiven. Our desire is to do the will of God, and to do the will of God is to love every creature in existence, and to love everything as God loves everything.

True Use of Kindness and Sympathy

The ordinary use of sympathy is responsible for a very large portion of the ills and the troubles we find in the world; the reason being that nearly all suffering is mental before it is physical, and that mental suffering is almost invariably produced when we enter into sympathetic touch with the ills that we meet among relations, friends or associates. The average person would suffer but little if he suffered only from the troubles that arise in his own system. It is the pain that is felt through sympathy for others that gives him most of the burdens he finds it necessary to bear. It is considered a sign of kindness, goodness and high regard, however, to sympathize with others in this manner, or rather to suffer with others, but this is not the true use of kindness.

We do not help others by entering into the same weakness that is keeping them in a world of distress. We do not help the weak by becoming weak. We do not relieve sickness by becoming sick. We do not right the wrong by entering into the wrong, or doing wrong. We do not free man from failures by permitting ourselves to become failures. We do not emancipate those who are in bondage to sin by going and committing the same sin. This is very simple; but ordinary sympathy is based upon the idea that we sympathize with a person only when we suffer with that person. We expect to relieve pain by proceeding to produce the same pain in our own systems; but we cannot remove darkness by entering into the dark We can remove wrong only by removing the cause of that wrong, and to remove the cause of wrong we must produce the cause of right. Darkness disappears when we produce light; likewise, sickness and trouble will vanish when we produce health and harmony, but we cannot produce health and harmony by entering into disease and trouble. This, however, is what ordinary sympathy does; it has, therefore, failed to relieve the world. The ordinary use of sympathy multiplies suffering by making suffering contagious. It causes the suffering of the one to give pain to the many, and then in turn causes the pain of the many to give additional pain to each individual person whose sympathy is aroused in the same connection. We must remove everything that tends to make ills contagious, whether it is physical or mental, and it is very evident that ordinary sympathy does spread pains and ills to a very great degree. Therefore, one of the first essentials in producing emancipation or in making real the ideal is to find the true use of sympathy. Sympathy itself must not be removed, because it is one of the highest virtues of the soul. The average person, however, misapplies this virtue continuously, and in consequence brings pains and ills both to himself and others, that could easily have been prevented. There is a better use for sympathy, and through this better use we cause all the good things in life to become contagious. Instead of entering into sympathetic touch with the weakness that may temporarily exist in the personality of man we enter into sympathetic touch with the strength that permanently exists in the soul of man. Instead of morbidly dwelling upon the ills and the wrongs which we find we proceed to gain the highest possible realization of the good, the right, the superior and the beautiful that we know has existence back of and above the superficial life of human nature. According to a metaphysical law, when we enter into mental contact with the good in man we awaken the power of that which is good in man, and the most perfect mental contact is produced by sympathy.

To sympathize with the soul is to increase the active power of the soul, because we always arouse into greater action that with which we sympathize, and when the active power of the soul is increased the weakness of the personality will become strength. To sympathize with the power of health and harmony in man will increase the power of health and harmony throughout his entire system and the elimination of sickness and trouble must inevitably follow. To sympathize with the pain a person may feel is to do nothing to relieve that person. You take the pain to yourself, but you do not take the pain away from the person with whom you sympathize. You thus double the suffering instead of removing it entirely, as you should. On the other hand, when we refuse to recognize the suffering itself and proceed to awaken in that person that something that can remove the suffering we protect ourselves from pain, while we actually do something to relieve that person from pain. We do not suffer with the person that suffers, but we do something to remove suffering absolutely from everybody concerned; instead of entering into the pain we take that person out of pain. That is sympathy that is sympathy. That is kindness that really results in a kind act. It does not weep, but does better. It removes both the cause and the effect of the weeping. It awakens that superior power in man that positively does produce emancipation. It does not cause suffering to be transmitted to a score of other persons who have done nothing to merit that suffering, but it stops the pain where it is and puts it out of existence absolutely.

Every form of suffering comes from the violation of some law in life. It is therefore wrong, but it cannot be righted by making a special effort to spread the results of that wrong among as many others as possible. This, however, ordinary sympathy does; it makes a special effort to make everybody feel bad because some one is not feeling as he should; but the pains of the many cannot give ease and comfort to the one, nor can many minds in bondage set one mind free. When any one is feeling bad it will not help him to have a group of morbid minds suffer with him. When any one is sorry it will not remove the cause of his grief to have others decide to be sorry also. Do something so that person will not feel bad any more. Take him out of his trouble. That is real sympathy; and while you are helping him out make him feel that your heart is as tender as tenderness itself. Do something so that the grief may be removed through the realization of that greater truth that knows that all is well. That is kindness worthy of the name.

Those, however, who are in the habit of sympathizing in the ordinary way may think the new way cold, and devoid of feeling or love, but the fact is that it is the ordinary form of sympathy that is devoid of love. When you love a person who is in pain you will not stand around and weep pretending that you are also feeling bad. You will put on the countenance of light and cheerfulness and actually do something tangible to remove his pain. That's love; and if you have real sympathy, you will minister to him with so much depth of feeling and tender kindness that you will touch the very innermost life of his soul. All love, all tenderness, all kindness and all real feeling come from the soul. Therefore, he whose sympathy is of the soul will receive his love and his kindness directly from the true source; in consequence, he will have more love and more kindness by far than the one whose sympathy is a form of morbid feeling.

The real purpose of true sympathy is twofold; first, to arouse in a greater measure that finer something in everybody with whom one may come in contact that will arouse this greater something, not only in others, but also in him who lives in this form of sympathy. In other words, to sympathize with the superior in man is to banish the wrong and the inferior by causing the expression of that divine something within that has the power to in life that is not only tender and sweet and beautiful, but is also immensely strong, strong with the strength of the Infinite; and second, to awaken everything in man that has quality, superiority and worth; that is, to make man feel the supreme power of his own inherent divinity. There is something in man that is greater than all weakness, all ills, all wrongs, and when this something is awakened, developed and expressed, all weakness, all ills and all wrongs must disappear. To sympathize with this greater something makes all things well. Such a sympathy will tend to build a stronger life, a better life, a superior life, a more beautiful life; and to give such a sympathy to everybody is kindness indeed.

There may seem to be kindness in weeping with those who weep, but it is a far greater kindness to give those people the power to banish their sorrows completely, and he who does this is not cold; he is the very essence of the highest and most beautiful love. There is no joy in having sorrow. There is no pleasure in having pain. Therefore, what greater good can man do for man than to help him gain complete emancipation from all those things, and this is the purpose of this higher use of sympathy. True sympathy is neither cold nor purely intellectual. It is real soul-feeling, while ordinary sympathy is simply a morbid mental feeling. True sympathy is the very fire of real spiritual love, because it springs from the very soul of love and is in constant touch with the unbounded power of that love. That such a sympathy should have extraordinary emancipating power is therefore most evident. The ordinary use of sympathy may appear to be kind. It may mean well, but it is usually misdirected kindness, and is nearly always weak. The higher use of sympathy, that is, the expression of divine sympathy, is not only kindness itself, but it has the spiritual understanding and the spiritual power to do what kindness wants to do. Ordinary kindness is usually crippled. It lacks both the power to do and the understanding to know what to do. The true sympathy, however, not only has the power to feel kindly, but has the power to act kindly. It not only gives love and makes everybody feel that they are in the presence of real love, but it also gives that something that can cause the purpose of love to come true. Real love invariably aims to produce comfort, peace and emancipation. That is its purpose, and real sympathy can fulfill that purpose. Therefore, this higher sympathy is the sympathy that is sympathy.

The same principle should be employed in the use of every form of emotion, because every emotion is a movement of the mind conveying mental elements and powers with certain definite objects in view. Therefore, the way the emotion acts will determine to a very great extent whether these mental powers will build for better things, or produce undesirable conditions. Those movements of the mind or emotions that express themselves in love, heartfelt joy and spiritual feeling have a beneficial effect; while that mental feeling that is usually termed emotionalism is never wholesome. True spiritual feeling is calm, but extremely beautiful and awakens orderly and harmoniously all the finer elements of human life. It is true spiritual feeling, or what may be termed emotions sublime, that gives action and expression to personal quality, mental worth and individual superiority. In other words, it is these actions of mind and soul that elevate thought, action, feeling, consciousness and desire above the planes of the ordinary. Such emotions should therefore be cultivated to the very highest and finest degree.

What is spoken of as heartfelt joy is that wholesome joy that comes directly from the heart and that has depth, reality and joyous feeling; but that joy that runs into uncontrolled ecstasy is never wholesome. Every feeling of joy that causes the mind to be carried away into excited or overwrought ecstasy is not joy, but mental intoxication. Such joy does not produce genuine happiness, and the reaction always disturbs the equilibrium of the wind. Depth of thought, clear thinking, intellectual brilliancy, good judgment, mental poise, all of these will diminish in the mind that indulges in uncontrolled ecstasy, emotionalism or pleasure that produces excitability and overwrought emotional feeling. The feeling of love, when it is love, is always wholesome and elevating, but passionate desire is weakening unless it is permeated through and through with genuine love. A deep, strong feeling of love will turn all desires, whether mental or physical, into constructive channels, but we must be certain that it is real love and not an artificial feeling temporarily produced by the misuse of the imagination. Here every mental movement that is intense, forced, overwrought or worked up to an abnormal pitch of excited enthusiasm leads to emotionalism, and emotionalism burns up energy. Nearly all kinds of nervous diseases can be traced directly or indirectly to emotionalism in one or more of its many forms; and as physical and mental weakness always follows the burning up of energy, a number of physical and mental ills can be traced to this source.

When emotionalism, fear, anger and worry are eliminated, all kinds of insanity and all kinds of nervous diseases will be things of the past; while the power, the capacity and the brilliancy of the average mind will increase to an extraordinary degree. Strong emotional feelings and intense enthusiasm will sometimes arouse a great deal of dormant, mental power. In consequence, people sometimes do exceptional things while under the emotional spell, but the entire process, as well as the final results, are very similar to that produced by alcoholic stimulants and other drugs. The system seems to be charged with a great deal of extra power for a while, but when the reaction comes the entire system becomes much weaker than it ever was before. The mind that permits itself to be aroused by intense, emotional feeling will gradually lose its power of clear thought. The understanding will become so weakened that the principles of real truth cannot be fully comprehended, while the judgment will follow more and more the illusions of an overwrought imagination. The fact that religious feeling among millions is so closely associated with this overwrought state of emotionalism proves the importance of a better understanding of the use of these finer mental elements. Emotionalism compels the mind to follow mere feeling, and mere feeling, when not properly blended with clear understanding, will be misdirected at every turn. Emotionalism also stupefies the finer perceptions by intoxicating the mind, and by burning up the finer mental energies; and since these finer perceptions are required to discern real truth we understand readily why highly emotional people cannot comprehend the principles of pure, spiritual metaphysics. Having been trained towards materialistic literalism instead of away from it, they are not to blame, however, for their present state and deserve no criticism. Nevertheless, those who wish to find real religion and real spirituality must learn to understand the psychology of emotion and must learn the true use of all the finer feelings of the mind.

There is something in man that is called religious feeling. It is present to a greater or lesser degree in everybody and cannot be removed, because it is a part of life itself. When in action, and it is never inactive very long, it expresses itself in some power of emotion. When this emotion or delicate mental movement is permitted to act without any definite purpose it becomes emotionalism; that is, mental energy running rampant, and becoming more and more intense until it destroys itself, as well as all the energy it originally contained. On the other hand, when this feeling is directed towards the highest and the most perfect conception of truth, life and being that the mind can possibly picture, all that is lofty, ideal and beautiful will be developed in the mind and soul of that individual. This is natural, because there is nothing that has greater developing power than deep, spiritual feeling; a fact that those who desire to develop remarkable ability, extraordinary talent and rare genius will do well to remember.

There is no mental faculty that is more readily affected by the emotions than the imagination, and since the imagination is such a very important faculty, no mental or physical action that in any way interferes with the constructive work of the imagination should be permitted. Emotionalism, however, invariably excites the imagination, and an excited imagination will imagine all sorts of things that are not true. The mind will thus be filled with illusions, and in consequence, false beliefs, wrong thoughts, perverted states and misdirected mental energy will follow. The result will be sickness, trouble, mistakes and failures in one or more of their many forms. It is now a well demonstrated truth that every thought has a definite power of its own, and, that power will produce its natural effect in some part of the human system. If the thought is not good the effect will naturally be undesirable, and conditions will be produced in mind or body that we do not want. But whatever we imagine, that we think; therefore, when we excite the imagination we imagine all manner of things that are untrue, unreal or abnormal; we produce false or perverted thought action in the mind; we think the wrong, and wrong thoughts invariably produce wrong conditions in mind or body, or both.

What we imagine we reproduce in ourselves to some degree, frequently to a marked degree; but an excited imagination simply cannot imagine what is good and wholesome. In every form of development, whether in the body, the mind or the soul, the imagining faculty is employed extensively. All growth is promoted by combining and recombining the elements of life in higher and higher forms, and since it is one of the functions of the imagination to produce these higher, more complex and more perfect combinations, development cannot take place unless the imagination works orderly, constructively and progressively. An excited imagination will produce false mental combinations or may waste energy by attempting to combine mental elements that will not combine. An orderly imagination may be likened to a skilled workman who builds a beautiful mansion out of his bricks, while an excited imagination might be likened to some one who can do nothing more than pile those bricks into a heap. The fact that emotionalism always excites the imagination proves therefore how impossible it is for minds with uncontrolled emotions to develop the greatness that is latent within them.

Another fact of great importance in this connection is that emotionalism will intensify every mental tendency that may be active in mind at the time. If there is a tendency towards abnormal desires, emotionalism will intensify those desires so that it will be very difficult to resist temptation should it appear. On the other hand, pure spiritual feeling would transmute those desires, and produce instead, an ascending tendency, thus leading all the forces of mind towards higher ground. To overcome emotionalism, intense mental feeling, anger, excitability and all overwrought or abnormal mental states, turn attention upon the spiritual heights of the soul whenever such mental feelings are felt. By training all mental feelings and emotions to move toward the deeper and the higher spiritual state of being these same feelings will become stronger, deeper, finer and more beautiful than they ever were before. We then establish the foundation upon which we can build an ideal character, and through such a character all the qualities of mind and soul can be used beneficially in the midst of every experience, whatever the nature of that experience may be.

To cause all the emotions to follow ascending tendencies will increase remarkably the power, the fineness, the life and the rapture of every phase of feeling, not only in the soul, but in the mind and the body as well. Every trace of coldness, indifference or lack of feeling will entirely disappear, and we shall develop instead that higher form of kindness, sympathy and spiritual emotion that is created in the likeness of divine emotion. Whoever employs this method will not permit his feelings to run wild at any time, but will cause the life and the power of every feeling to accumulate in his system. He will hold them all in poise and use their energies intelligently in the building up of his whole life and in adding to the joy, the rapture and the delight of the living of a full, strong, ever-ascending state of existence. That person who controls his feelings and turns all the energies of those feelings upon the spiritual heights of the soul will actually become a living flame of love, sympathy and sublime emotion. Such a person will enjoy everything intensely, but his joy will be in such a high state of harmony that he will waste nothing in his life; instead, all the elements and powers of his life will continue to accumulate, thus giving added strength, worth and superiority to everything that he may physically, mentally or spiritually possess.

Talk Health, Happiness and Prosperity

Talk happiness. When things look dark, talk happiness. When things look bright, talk more happiness. When others are sad, insist on being glad. Talk happiness, and they will soon feel better. Talk happiness; it pays in every shape and form and manner. Give sunshine to others, and others will be more than pleased to give sunshine to you. Talk happiness, and your health will be better, your mind will be brighter and your personality far more attractive; but the qualities that happiness will give to you will also be given to those who have the pleasure to listen to you when you talk happiness.

Talk happiness, and you will always remain in a happy frame of mind. You will encourage thousands of others to do the same. You will become a fountain of joy in the midst of the garden of human life, and who can tell how many flowers of kindness and joy unfolded their rare and tender beauty because you were there. When others have lost courage, talk happiness. The future is bright for everybody. Talk happiness, and you turn on the light in their pathway, and they will see the better things that are before them. When the mind is depressed it is blinded; it sees only the darkness; but when the light of joy is admitted, everything is changed. Therefore, talk happiness to all persons and on all occasions.

We cannot have too much light in the world, and the more we talk happiness the more light we produce wherever we may be. What greater pleasure could anyone desire than to realize that he has eased the way of life for thousands and sent the sunbeams and joy into the mental world of tens of thousands? You can do this by talking happiness. Thus by constantly talking happiness you produce perpetual increase in your own happiness. What we give in abundance always returns in abundance; that is, when we give in the right spirit; and he who talks happiness is always in the right spirit. When in the midst of discord, trouble or confusion, talk happiness. Harmony will soon be restored. The majority can easily change their minds for the better when some one takes the lead. You can take the lead by talking happiness.

Talk prosperity. When times are not good, man himself must make them better, and he can make them better by doing his best and having faith in that power that produces prosperity. When men have faith in prosperity they will think prosperity, live prosperity and thus do that which produces prosperity; and you can give men faith in prosperity by constantly talking prosperity.

They may not listen at first, but perseverance always wins. Prosperity is extremely attractive, and the more you impress it upon the minds of others the more attractive it becomes until no one can resist it; and when we admit the idea of prosperity into our own minds we will from that moment begin to produce prosperity. Think prosperity, talk prosperity, and live prosperity; and you will rise in the scale no matter what the circumstances may be. Hold to the power that produces abundance by having unbounded faith in that power and you will overcome all adversity and reach the highest goal you have in view. The fear of failure produces more failure than all other causes combined. You can remove that fear by talking prosperity.

Talk health. It is the best medicine. When people stop talking sickness they will stop getting sick. Talk health and stay well. Talk health to the person who is sick and you will cause him to think health. He who thinks health will live health, and he who lives health will produce health. When your associates take delight in relating minutely everything they know about the ills of the community, purify the muddy waters of their conversation by talking health. Insist on talking health. Prove that there is more health than sickness, and that therefore health is the more important subject. The majority rules. Health is in the majority. Increase that majority by talking more health. Take the lead in this manner of conversation, and be positively determined to continue in the lead. Others will soon follow, and when they do, sickness will diminish more and more until it becomes practically unknown among those who have the privilege to live in your circle.

When the sins of the world are in evidence, talk virtue. When the power of virtue is in evidence, talk more virtue. Eternally emphasize the good; give it more and more power, and it will soon become sufficiently strong to produce that ideal of power that you wish to make real. Talk virtue, and people will think of virtue; they will dwell more and more upon the beauty of virtue. Ere long they will desire virtue, and that desire will become stronger and stronger until it thrills every atom in human life. To desire virtue is to become virtuous. To live for the attainment of purity is to place in action all the purifying elements in your being, and you will soon realize that perfectly clean condition that every awakened mind has learned to worship. You can purify the minds of thousands by constantly talking virtue, and these thousands will in turn convey the power of virtue to as many thousand times thousands more.

Talk virtue eternally and there is no end to the good that you may do. When the world seems bad, talk virtue. The power of good is not gone; it is just as great as it ever was, and it is here and there and everywhere. You can open the mind of man to the mighty influx of this power by eternally talking virtue. You can, through the proper use of your own words, change the tide of human thought. You can cause all mankind to desire virtue by forever talking virtue. On the surface many things may seem to be what they ought not to be, but the surface is not all there is. It is an insignificant part of the whole. There is a hidden richness in life that the many do not see, because their attention has never been turned in that direction. You can lead mankind into the gold mines of the mind and into the diamond fields of the soul, and the secret lies in the words you speak. You can guide the mind of man by the way you talk. Talking therefore should not be empty, but should ever have a sublime goal in view. Your words point the way and they who hear what you have to say will, to some degree, be influenced to go whatever way your words may point. Your power, therefore, in directing other minds towards greater and better things is hidden in every word you speak, and how important that this power be wisely employed.

We are responsible for every word we express. It will affect somebody either for good or otherwise. Talk sin, sickness and trouble, and you will cause many to go directly into more sin, sickness and trouble. Talk health, happiness and prosperity, and you will cause many to find health, happiness and prosperity in greater and greater abundance. When the world complains, do not forget to emphasize the great fact that universal good is even now at hand. The complaining mind wears colored glasses. He cannot see things as they are. You can help him to remove those glasses by calling his attention to the fact that things are not what they seem to him. Everything lies in the point of view. Look at things from the right point of view and you will be happy, cheerful and optimistic under all sorts of circumstances. But look at things from the wrong point of view, and you will see nothing clearly; everything will appear to be what it is not. You will thus live in confusion and your mistakes will be many. Remove this confusion by placing yourself in harmony with eternal good, and you can do this by talking about the good, thinking about the good and emphasizing most positively every expression of good with which you may come in contact. That which we think of and talk of constantly will multiply and grow in our own world.

Talk peace. You will thus not only prevent confusion, but you will remove those confused conditions that may already exist. You can still the storms of life everywhere by talking peace. When man thinks the most of peace he will be in peace, and he cannot fail to think of peace so long as he is faithfully talking peace. Talk success, and you will inspire everybody with the spirit of success. You will help to turn the energies of life upon the goal of success, and thus you will help all minds to move towards success. Never say that anything is impossible. Talk success, and you help to make everything possible. Everybody should succeed. It is not only the privilege of everybody to succeed, but every person, to be just to himself, must succeed. The fear of failure, however, is the greatest obstacle. You can remove that fear by talking success. Hold the idea of success before every mind with which you come in contact; you will thus become one of the greatest philanthropists in the world.

New and greater opportunities may be found everywhere. Talk of these things and forget the missteps of the past. We can leave the lesser that is behind only by pressing on towards the greater that is before. Talk success to everybody, and everybody will press on towards the greater goal of success. Be an inspiration among all minds; and you can be by holding up the light of success, prosperity and attainment at all times. Use your words in promoting advancement, in awakening new interest in the better side, the brighter side, the sunny side, and turn the mind of man upon those things that can be done. He can who thinks he can, and you help every person to think that he can by talking prosperity and success. Impress the greater upon every mind, and every mind will think the greater; and he who thinks the greater is constantly building for greater things. Emphasize the sunny side in all your speech and you provide a never failing antidote for complaints; and since the complaining mind soon becomes the retrogressing mind, this antidote has extreme value. It may change for the better the destiny of anyone when brought squarely before his attention, and this your words can do.

When one door closes another opens; sometimes several. This is the law of life. It is the expression of the law of eternal progress. The whole of nature desires to move forward eternally. The spirit of progress animates everything. Whenever a person loses an opportunity to move forward this great law proceeds to give him another. This proves that the universe is kind, that everything is for man and nothing against him. This being the truth, the man who talks health, happiness, prosperity, power and progress is working in harmony with the universe, and is helping to promote the great purpose of the universe; and who would not occupy a position of such value and importance? Whenever you talk trouble, failure, sickness or sin you arraign your own mind against the law of life and the purpose of the universe. You will thereby be against everything, and everything will, in consequence, be against you. You must, therefore, necessarily fail in everything you undertake to do. But how different everything will be when you turn and move in the other direction. Go with the universe, and all the power of the universe will go with you, and will help you to reach whatever object you may have is view.

Harmonize yourself with the laws of life and you will steadily rise in the scale of life. Nothing can hold you down. Everything you undertake to do you will accomplish, because everything will be with you. You will reach every ideal, and at the best time and under the best circumstances cause that ideal to become real. When you cease to talk failure and begin to talk success you invariably meet the turn in the lane. You find that a new world and a better future is in store. Things will take a turn when you take a turn, and you will take a turn when you begin to talk about those things that you desire to realize. Never talk about anything else. The way you talk you go. The way you talk others will go. Therefore, talk health, happiness and prosperity, and help everybody, yourself included, to move towards health, happiness and prosperity. The power of words is immense, both in the person that speaks and in the person that is spoken to. The simplest way to use this power is to train yourself to talk the things you want; talk the things that you expect or desire to realize; talk the things you wish to attain and accomplish. You thus cause the power of words to work for you and with you in gaining the goal you have in mind. Whatever comes, talk health, happiness and prosperity. Say that you are well; say that you are happy; say that you are prosperous. Emphasize everything that is good in life, and the power of the Supreme will cause your words to come true.

What Determines the Destiny of Man

The destiny of every individual is being hourly created by himself, and what he is to create at any particular time is determined by those ideals that he entertains at that time. The future of a person is not preordained by some external power, nor is fate controlled by some strange, mysterious force that masterminds alone can comprehend and employ. It is ideals that control fate, and all minds have their ideals wherever in the scale of life they may be. To have ideals is not simply to have dreams or visions of that which lies beyond the attainments of the present; nor is idealism a system of ideas that the practical mind may not have the privilege to entertain. To have ideals is to have definite objects in view, be those objects very high or very low, or anywhere between those extremes.

The ideals of any mind are the real wants, the real desires or the real aims of that mind, and as every normal mind invariably lives, thinks and works for that which is wanted by his present state of existence, it is evident that every mind must necessarily, either consciously or unconsciously, follow his ideals. When those ideals are low, ordinary or inferior the individual will work for the ordinary and the inferior, and the products of his mind will correspond in quality with that for which he is working. Inferior causes will originate in his life and similar effects will follow; but when those ideals are high and superior, he will work for the superior; he will develop superiority in himself, and he will give superiority to everything that he may produce. Every action that he originates in his life will become a superior cause and will be followed by a similar effect.

The destiny of every individual is determined by what he is and by what he does; and what any individual is to be or do is determined by what he is living for, thinking for or working for. Man is not being made by some outside force. Man is making himself with the power of those forces and elements that he employs in his thought and his work; and in all his efforts, physical or mental, he invariably follows his ideals. He who lives, thinks and works for the superior becomes superior; he who works for less, becomes less. It is therefore evident that any individual may become more, achieve more, secure more and create for himself a greater and a greater destiny by simply beginning to live, think and work for a superior group of ideals. To have low ideals is to give the creative forces of the system something ordinary to work for. To have high ideals is to give those forces something extraordinary to work for, and the fate of man is the result of what his creative forces hourly produce. Every force in the human system is producing something, and that something will become a part of the individual. It is therefore evident that any individual can constantly improve the power, the quality and the worth of his being by directing the forces of his system to produce that which has quality and worth. These forces, however, are not directed or controlled by the will. It is the nature of the creative forces in man to produce what the mind desires, wants, needs or aspires to attain, and the desires and the aspirations of any mind are determined by the ideals that are entertained in that mind.

The forces of the system will begin to work for the superior when the mind begins to attain superior ideals, and since it is the product of these forces that determines both the nature and the destiny of man, a superior nature and a greater destiny may be secured by any individual who will adopt the highest and the most perfect system of idealism that he can possibly comprehend. To entertain superior ideals is to picture in mind and to hold constantly before mind the highest conception that can be formed of everything of which we may be conscious. To mentally dwell in those higher conceptions at all times is to cause the predominating ideas to become superior ideas, and it is the predominating ideas for which we live, think and work. When the ruling ideas of any mind are superior the creative force of that mind will produce the superior in every element, faculty, talent or power in that mind; greatness will thus be developed in that mind, and the great mind invariably creates a great destiny.

To entertain superior ideals is not to dream of the impossible, but to enter into mental contact with those greater possibilities that we are now able to discern; and to have the power to discern an ideal indicates that we have the power to realize that ideal. We do not become conscious of greater possibilities until we have developed sufficient capacity to work out those possibilities into practical, tangible results. Therefore, when we discern the greater we are ready to attain and achieve the greater; but before we can proceed to do what we are ready to do we must adopt superior ideals, and superior ideals only. When our ideals are superior we shall constantly think of the superior, because as our ideals are so is our thinking, and to constantly think of the superior is to steadily grow into the likeness of the superior. When the ideals are very high all the forces of the system will move towards superior attainments; all things in the life of the individual will work together with greater and greater greatness in view, and continued advancement on a larger and larger scale must inevitably follow. To entertain superior ideals is not simply to desire some larger personal attainment or to mentally dwell in some belief that is different from the usual beliefs of the world. To entertain superior ideals is to think the very best thoughts and the very greatest thoughts about everything with which we come in contact. Superior idealism is not mere dreaming of the great and the beautiful, but is actual living in mental harmony with the very best we can find in all things, in all persons, in all circumstances and in all expressions of life. To live in mental harmony with the best we can find everywhere is to create the best in our own mentality and personality; and as we steadily grow into the likeness of that which we think of the most, we will, through ideal thinking, perpetually increase our power, capacity and worth. In consequence, we will naturally create a greater and a more worthy destiny.

The man who becomes much will achieve much, and great achievements invariably build a great destiny. To think of anything that is less than the best, or to mentally dwell with the inferior is to neutralize the effect of those superior ideals that we have begun to entertain. To secure the greatest results it is therefore absolutely necessary to entertain superior ideals only and to cease all recognition of inferiority or imperfection. The reason why the majority fail to secure any tangible results from higher ideals is because they entertain too many of the lower ideals at the same time. They may aim high; they may adore the beautiful; they may desire the perfect; they may live for the better and work for the greater, but they do not think their best thoughts about everything, and this is the reason why they do not reach the goal they have in view. Some of their forces are building for greater things, while other forces are building for lesser things, and a house divided against itself cannot stand.

Superior idealism contains no thought that is less than the very greatest and the very best that the most lofty states of mind can possibly produce, and it entertains no desire that has not the very greatest worth, the greatest power, and the highest attainment in view. Superior idealism does not recognize the power of evil in anything or in anybody; it knows that adverse conditions exist, but it gives the matter no conscious thought whatever. It is not possible to think the greatest thought about everything while mind is giving conscious attention to adversity or imperfection. The true idealist, therefore, gives conscious recognition to the power of good only, and he lives in the conviction that all things in his life are constantly working together for good. This conviction is not mere sentiment with the idealist. He knows that all things positively will work together for good when we recognize only the good, think only the good, desire only the good and expect only the good; likewise, he knows that all things positively will work together for greater things when all the powers of life, thought and action are concentrated upon the attainment and the achievement of greater things.

To apply the principles of superior idealism in all things means advancement in all things. To follow the superior ideal is to move towards the higher, the greater and the superior, and no one can continue very long in that movement without creating for himself a new world, a better environment and a greater destiny. To create a better future begin now to select a better group of ideals. Select the best and the greatest ideals that you can possibly find, and live those ideals absolutely. You will thus cause everything in your being to work for the higher, the better and the greater, and the things that you work for now will determine what the future is to be. Work for the greatest and the best that you know in the present, and you will create the very greatest and the very best for the future.

To Him That Hath Shall Be Given

The statement that much gathers more is true on every plane of life and in every sphere of existence; and the converse that every loss leads to a greater loss is equally true; though we must remember that man can stop either process at any time or place. The further down you go the more rapidly you will move towards the depths, and the higher up you go the easier it becomes to go higher still. When you begin to gain you will gain more, because "To him that hath shall be given." When you begin to lose you will lose more, because from "Him that hath not, even that which he hath shall be taken away." This is a great metaphysical law, and being metaphysical, man has the power to use it in any way that he may desire. As man is in the within, so everything will be in his external world. Therefore, whether man is to lose or gain in the without depends upon whether he is losing or gaining in the within.

The basis of all possession is found in the consciousness of man, and not in exterior circumstances, laws or conditions. If a man's consciousness is accumulative, he will positively accumulate, no matter where he may live; but whether his riches are to be physical, intellectual or spiritual will depend upon the construction of his mind. When the mind has the greatest development on the physical plane an accumulative consciousness will gather tangible possessions. When the mind has the greatest development on the intellectual or metaphysical plane, an accumulative consciousness will gather abundance of knowledge and wisdom. When the mind has the greatest development on the spiritual plane an accumulative consciousness will gather spiritual riches. However competent you may be on the physical plane, if your consciousness is not accumulative, you will not gain possession of a great deal of this world's goods. Likewise, no matter how diligently you may search for wisdom in the higher spiritual possessions, if your consciousness is not accumulative you will gain but little. In fact, you will constantly lose the knowledge of truth on the one hand while trying to gain it on the other. Therefore, to gain abundance in the world of things or tangible possessions, the secret is to become competent in our chosen vocations, and then acquire an accumulative consciousness.

To gain the riches of the mind and the soul, the secret is to develop the same accumulative consciousness and to consecrate all the powers of mind and thought to spiritual things. There are thousands in this age who have consecrated their whole lives to the higher state of being, but there are very few who have gained the real riches of the spiritual kingdom, and the reason is they have neglected the development of the accumulative consciousness. In other words, they have overlooked the great law, "To him that bath shall be given." Those who have nothing will receive nothing, no matter how devotedly they may pray or how beautifully they may live. But to have is not simply to possess in the external sense. Those who are conscious of nothing have nothing. Those who are conscious of much have much, regardless of external possession. Before we can gain anything we must have something, and to have something is to be conscious of something.

We must be conscious of possession in the within before we can increase possession in any sphere of existence. All possession is based upon consciousness and is held by consciousness or lost by consciousness. All gain is the result of an accumulative consciousness. All loss is due to what may be termed the scattering consciousness; that is, that state of consciousness that lets go of everything that may come within its sphere. When you are conscious of something you are among those that hath and to you shall be given more. As soon as you gain conscious hold of things you will begin to gain possession of more and more things. As soon as you gain conscious hold upon wisdom and spiritual power, wisdom and spiritual power will be given to you in greater and greater abundance. On the other hand, when you begin to lose conscious hold of things, thoughts or powers, you will begin to lose more and more of those possessions, until all are gone.

When you inwardly feel that things are slipping away from you, you are losing your conscious hold of things, and all will finally be lost if you do not change your consciousness. When you inwardly feel that you are gaining more and more, or that things are beginning to gravitate towards your sphere of existence, more and more will be given to you until you have everything that you may desire. How we feel in the within is the secret, and it is this interior feeling that determines whether we are to be among those that have or among those that have not. When you feel in the within that you are gaining more you are among those that have, and to you shall be given more. When you feel in the within that you are losing what you have, you are among those that have not, and from you shall be taken away even that which you have.

When we learn that mind is cause and that everything we gain may come from the action of mind as cause, we discover that all possession is dependent upon the attitude of mind, and since we have the power to hold the mind in any attitude desired, all the laws of gain and possession are in our own hands. When this discovery is made we begin to gain conscious possession of ourselves, and to him that hath himself all other things shall be given. To feel that you, yourself, are the power behind other powers, and that you may determine what is to come and what is to go, is to become conscious of the fact that you are something. You thus become conscious of something in yourself that is real, that is substantial and that is actually supreme in your world. To become conscious of something in yourself is to have something, and to have something is to gain more; consequently, by gaining consciousness of that something that is real in yourself you become one of those that hath and to you shall be given.

To gain consciousness of the real in yourself is to gain consciousness of the real in life, and the more you feel the reality of life the more real life becomes. The result is that your consciousness of the reality of life becomes larger and larger; it comprehends more and takes in more. In other words, it is becoming accumulative. When this realization is attained you gain conscious hold upon life and are gradually gaining conscious hold upon everything that exists in life. This means a greater and greater mastery of life, and mastery is always followed by an increase in possession. Whatever you become conscious of in yourself, that you gain possession of in yourself. Whatever you gain possession of in yourself, that you can constructively employ in your sphere of existence, and whatever is constructively employed is productive; it produces something. Therefore, by becoming conscious of something you gain the power to produce something, and products on any plane constitute riches on that plane.

The more you become conscious of in yourself and in your life the greater your power to create and produce in your sphere of action, and the more wealth you produce the greater your possession, providing you have learned how to retain the products of your own talent. When we analyze these laws from another point of view we find the consciousness of the real in ourselves produces an ascending tendency in the mind, and whenever the mind begins to go up, the law of action and reaction will continue to press the mind up further and further indefinitely. Every upward action of mind, produces a reaction that pushes the mind upward still farther. As the mind is pushed upward a second upward action is expressed that is stronger than the first; this in turn produces a second reaction stronger than the first reaction, and the mind is pushed upward the second time much farther than it was the first time. The fact is, when the mind enters the ascending scale the law of action and reaction will perpetuate the ascension so long as the mind takes a conscious interest in the progress made; but the moment the mind loses interest in the movement the law will reverse itself and the mind enters the descending scale. Therefore, become conscious of the law in yourself and take a conscious interest in every step in advance that you make, and you will go up in the scale of life continually and indefinitely.

When the mind is in the ascending scale it is steadily becoming larger, more powerful and more competent, and will consequently be in demand where recompense is large and the opportunities more numerous. Such a mind will naturally gain step by step in rapid succession. To such a mind will be given more and more continually, because it has placed itself in the world of those who have. The great secret of gaining more, regardless of circumstances, is to continue perpetually to go up in mind. No matter how things are going about you, continue to go up in mind. Every upward step that is taken in mind adds power to mind, and this added power will produce added results in the tangible world. When these added results are observed mind gains more faith in itself, and more faith always brings more power. On the other hand, when we permit ourselves to go down in mind, because things seem to go down, we lose power. This loss of power will prevent us from doing our work properly or from using those things and conditions about us to the best advantage. In consequence, things will actually go down more and more; and if we permit this losing of ground to make us still more discouraged, we lose still more power, to be followed by still more adversity and loss. It is therefore evident that the way we go in mind everything in our world will go also, and that if we change our minds and stay changed, everything else will change and stay changed. If we continue to go up in mind, never permitting retrogression for a moment, everything in our world will continue to go up, and there will not even be signs of reverse, much less the loss of anything which we wish to retain.

When things seem to go wrong we should stay right and continue to stay right, and things will soon decide to come and be right also. This is a law that works and never fails to work. When we permit ourselves to go wrong because things seem to go wrong, we produce what may be termed the letting go attitude of mind, and when we cease to hold on to things, things will begin to slip away. We must hold on to things ourselves, if we wish to retain them for ourselves; and the secret of holding on to things is to continue positively in that attitude of mind that is perpetually going up into the larger and the greater. The laws of life will continue perpetually to give to those who have placed themselves in the receiving attitude, and those same laws will take away from those who have placed themselves in the losing attitude. When you create a turn in yourself you will feel that things are also taking a turn to a degree; and if you continue persistently in this feeling, everything in your life will positively take the turn that you have taken. As you go everything in your world will go, providing you continue to go; the law of action and reaction explains why. In the last analysis, however, everything depends upon whether consciousness determines how every force, element, power or faculty is to act, because they are all controlled by consciousness. When your consciousness does not have the proper hold on things, the power of your being will fail to gain the proper hold on things; but when your consciousness does possess this holding power, all the powers of your being will gain the same firm grip upon everything with which they may have to deal.

To establish the accumulative consciousness, that is, that consciousness that has complete hold on things, train yourself to inwardly feel that you have full possession of everything in your own being. Feel that you possess yourself. Affirm that you possess yourself. Think constantly of yourself as possessing yourself, everything that is in yourself, and you will soon be conscious of absolute self-possession. Some have this conscious feeling naturally, and they invariably gain vast possessions, either in tangible goods or in wisdom and higher spiritual powers. But every one can develop this state of conscious possession of his whole self by remaining firm in the conviction that "All that I am is mine." When you begin to feel that you possess yourself you actually have something in consciousness, and according to the laws of gain and possessions you will gain more and more without end. You are in the same consciousness with those who have, and to you will be given. You have established the inner cause of possession through the conscious possession of your entire inner life, and the effect of this cause, that is, the perpetual increase of external possession, must invariably follow. In brief, you have applied the great law "To Him That Hath Himself All Other Things Shall Be Given".

The Life That is Worth Living

To the average person life means but little, because he has not discovered the greater possibilities of his real existence. He has been taught to think that to make a fortune or to make a name for himself are the only things worth while, and if he does not happen to have the necessary talent for these accomplishments there is nothing much else for him to do but to merely exist. However, if he has been touched with the force of ambition, or if he has had a glimpse of the ideal, mere existence does not satisfy, and the result is a life of unhappiness and dissatisfaction. But such a person must learn that there are other openings and opportunities in life besides mere existence, regardless of what the mental capacity of the individual may be. These other opportunities, when taken advantage of, will give just as much happiness, if not more, than what is secured by those who have won the admiration of the world; besides, when one learns to live for these other things real living becomes a fine art, and he begins to live a life that is really worth while. There is many a person whose present position in life depends almost wholly upon his financial returns, and if these are small, with no indications of immediate increase, his life seems to be almost, if not wholly, a barren waste; not because it is a barren waste, but because he has not found the real riches of existence. The trouble with this person is the point of view; he is depending upon things instead of depending upon himself. He must learn that there is something more to live for besides his salary and what his salary can buy. The value of the individual life is not measured by the quantity of possessions, but by the quality of existence. The value of life comes not from having much, but from being much; and happiness is invariably a state of mind coming, not from what a person has, but from what he is. We must remember, however, that he who is much will finally gain much, providing the powers in his possession are practically applied; and his gains will have high quality whether they be gains in the world of things or in the world of mind, consciousness and soul.

The problem for the average person to solve is what he actually can do with himself in his present position. He may not be earning much now, and his opportunities for earning more may not be clearly in evidence, but he is nevertheless living in a great sea of opportunities, many of which may be taken advantage of at once. The first of these is the opportunity to make of himself a great personality, and in taking advantage of this opportunity he should remember that to do great things in the world is not the only thing worth while. To be great in the world is of equal if not greater worth, and he who is now becoming great in his own life will, without fail, do great things in years to come. The majority of those who have practical capacity are making strenuous efforts to do something great, something startling, that will arrest the attention of the world; while those who do not possess this practical capacity are not satisfied because they are not similarly favored. In the meantime neither class gains happiness, and the best forces of life are employed in the making of things, most of which are valueless, while the making of great personalities is postponed to some future time.

The capacity to make great things is not the only capacity of value in the possession of man; but all minds do not possess this capacity; all minds, however, do possess the power to remake themselves in the exact likeness of all that is great and beautiful and ideal. Begin now to rebuild your own personality and proceed in the realization of the fact that you have the power to produce an edition Deluxe out of your own present personal self. You could hardly find a purpose of greater interest and of greater possibility than this, and results will be secured from the very beginning. To find your own personality passing through a transformation process, bringing out into expression the finest and the best that you can picture in your ideals, is something that will add immensely to the joy and the worth of living. In fact, this alone would make life not only worth living, but so rich that every moment would become a source of unbounded satisfaction in itself.

The average person usually asks himself how much money he can make during the next ten years, but why should he not ask himself how much happiness he can enjoy during those same years, or how much brilliancy he can develop in his mind, or how much more beautiful he may become in body, character and soul? He would find that by living for these latter things he would not only perpetually enrich his life and live a life that is thoroughly worth living, but he would find that the earning of money would become much easier than if he simply lived for material gain alone. The ambition of the average person is to do something great in the world of things; but why is he not ambitious to do something great in the perfecting of his own being, the most wonderful world in the universe? Such ambitions are truly worth living for and working for, but our attention has not been called to their extraordinary possibilities; therefore, we have neglected the greater while wasting most of our energies on the lesser.

There are a number of ambitions outside of the usual ones that could engage our attention with the greatest of profit, because they not only have worth in themselves, but they lead to so many other things that have worth. The desire to secure as much out of life as life can possibly give will not only make living intensely interesting, but the more life a person can live the more power he will get. Live a great life and you gain great power. The increase of your power will enable you to carry out a number of other ambitions, thus adding to the richness of your life from almost every imaginable source. When a person declares that his greatest ambition is to live he is taking the most interesting, the most satisfying, the most profitable and the most complete course in life that can possibly be selected. Living, itself, when made a fine art, is one continuous feast, and the fact that all increase of power comes from the increase of life makes the ambition to live not only the greatest ambition of all, but the means through which all other ambitions may be realized.

If your present life does not hold as much as you would wish, do not think of it as an empty state of existence. Do not depend upon those few things that you are receiving from the external world; but begin to draw upon the limitless life and power that exists in the vastness of your interior world. Then you will find something to live for. Then you will begin to live a life that is thoroughly worth while. Then you will find the real riches of existence, and you will also find that these riches will so increase your personal power and worth that you will become able to take advantage of those opportunities that lead to things of tangible worth.

When the world of things does not seem to hold any new opportunities for you resolve to grow more and more beautiful in body, character and soul with the passing of the years. Make this your ambition, and if you do your utmost to carry out this ambition, you will gain far more satisfaction from its realization than if you had amassed an immense fortune. Live to express in body, mind and soul all that is high and beautiful and ideal in your sublime nature, and you will not only give yourself unbounded joy, but you will become a great inspiration to the entire world. The life that is not expressed through the beautiful nor surrounded by the beautiful is not worth a great deal to the mind of man; but there is practically no end to the joy and richness that man may gain through that which is actually beautiful. The beautiful not only gives happiness, but it opens the mind of man to those higher realms from which proceed all that is worthy or great or ideal. To look upon the beautiful is to gain glimpses of that vast transcendent world where supreme life is working out the marvelous destiny of man. Therefore, there can be no greater ambition than to live for the purpose of giving higher and more ideal expression to the life of that sublime world.

To give expression in personal life to the great riches of the interior world is worth far more, both to yourself and to the race, than it is to gain possession of any number of things in the external world. The man who simply gains wealth never gains happiness; besides, he is soon forgotten. But the man who will live for the purpose of giving expression to mental and spiritual wealth will gain unlimited happiness, and his life will be so illustrious that his name will never be forgotten. And remember that no matter how insignificant your position in life may be today, or how small your income, or how limited your opportunities, you can begin this moment to give expression to the vast riches of your interior life; and before you take your departure from this sphere you may become such a great light in the world of higher illumined attainment that your accomplishments in this unique sphere of action will continue to inspire the world for ages yet to come.

To live for the purpose of developing the gold mines of the mind and the diamond fields of the soul, are ambitions that might engage the attention of millions who have found no satisfaction in the world of things; and to those who will make these their leading ambitions a rich future is certainly in store; and, in addition, the present will be filled to overflowing with almost everything that can give interest and happiness to life. To develop a charming personality, to live a long life, to live a happy life, and to retain your health, your youth and your vigor as long as you live, these are ambitions that anyone can work for with the greatest interest and profit; and to him who will accomplish these things the world will give more honor than it has given to its greatest musicians, its most brilliant orators or its most illustrious statesmen.

To live for the purpose of unfolding the latent powers of your being is a work that will not only prove interesting to an exceptional degree, but will prove exceedingly rich in future possibilities. That there is practically no end to the possibilities that are latent in man is now the firm conviction of all real psychologists. Therefore, we need not weep because there are no more worlds to conquer. We are on the borderland of greater worlds than were ever dreamed of by the most illumined seers that the world has ever known. We need not feel discouraged because our position in life seems uninteresting or insignificant. We have opportunities at our very door that are so great and so numerous that it will require an eternity to take advantage of them all. Though the external world may not as yet have given us much to live for, the internal world stands ready to lavish upon us so much that is rich and marvelous that not a single moment need be otherwise than a feast fit for the gods. The doors of this internal world are open, and he who will walk in will begin to live a life that is great, indeed.

When we look into life as life really is there is so much to live for and there is so much to accomplish and attain that even eternity seems too short. The problem to solve is to know the greatest thing we can do now; and the solution may be found by resolving to live for that which is nearest at hand, whatever that may be. Accept the greatest opportunity that you can take advantage of now, and then begin to live for the working out of everything that that opportunity may contain. Do not long for opportunities that are out of reach. The majority do this and thus waste their time. Do not wait for opportunities to do great things. The opportunity to make of yourself a great soul, a marvelous mind and a higher developed personality is at hand, and by taking advantage of this opportunity you will awaken within yourself those powers that can do great things. You will thus cause your present to become all that you may wish it to be; you will build for a future that which will be nothing less than extraordinary; and you will be living a life that is thoroughly worth living in the great eternal now. You will be making the ideal real at every step of the way, but every moment will lead you into worlds that are richer and realms that are fairer than you ever dreamed of before. It is therefore evident that when we learn to live the life that is really worth living, there is no reason whatever why a single moment should be empty, dull or uninteresting in the life of any person, because there is so much to live for that has real worth, so much to enjoy that holds real enjoyment, so much to do that is thoroughly worth doing; besides, the whole of life, when actually lived, is eternally alive with interest, ever revealing the splendor of its vast transcendent domains. And he who aims to live for the purpose of gaining the realization of, and the possession of, as many spheres of this life as possible will find full expression for every ambition and every aspiration that he can possibly arouse in his mind. Life to him will be a continuous feast and existence will become an endless advancement into the highest attainments and the greater achievements that even the most illustrious mind can picture as its goal.

When All Things Become Possible

When the mind is placed in conscious contact with the limitless powers of universal life all things become possible, and faith is the secret. To have faith is to possess that interior insight through which we can discern the marvelous possibilities that are latent in the great within, and to possess the power to enter into the very life of the great within. To most minds there seems to be a veil in consciousness between the spheres of present understanding and the spheres of the higher wisdom, and though there are many who feel distinctly that there is something greater within them, yet it seems hidden, and they cannot discern it. Faith, however, has the power to perceive those greater things within that previously seemed hidden, and this is the reason why faith is the evidence of things not seen. Faith does not simply believe. It knows; it knows through higher insight, because faith is this higher insight. Faith is not blind, objective belief, but a higher development of consciousness through which the mind transcends the circumscribed and enters into the life of the boundless.

When faith is active consciousness is expanded so much that it breaks all bounds and penetrates even those realms that objective man has never heard of before. In this way new truth and discoveries are brought to light, and this is how man gains the understanding of what previously seemed to be beyond his comprehension. When we define faith as that power in mind through which consciousness can penetrate into the larger sphere of life we perceive readily why almost anything can be accomplished through faith, and we also understand why no one can afford to work without faith. When consciousness enters a larger sphere of action its capacity is naturally increased, and the greater power that can be drawn upon in performing any kind of work increases in proportion; likewise, the knowing how to work will be promoted in the same manner. To do anything successfully one must know how to do it and have the power to do what one knows should be done, and both these essentials are increased in proportion to the enlargement of consciousness. One of the principal metaphysical laws declares that whatever you become conscious of you express through your personality; therefore, according to this law more life, more power and more wisdom will come into actual possession in the personal life as we become conscious of more and more of these things in the mental life; in other words, the ideal is made real.

The art of extending consciousness into the realms of unlimited life and power and wisdom is the secret through which all great attainments and great achievements become possible; but without faith this enlargement of consciousness cannot take place, because faith is that power that perceives and enters into the greater things that are still before us. Faith looks into the beyond of every faculty, talent or power and perceives that there is much more of these same talents and powers further on. In fact, there is no visible limit to anything when viewed through the eyes of faith. Consciousness does not extend itself in any direction until it feels that there will be tangible grounds upon which to proceed. You can become conscious only of those things that seem real; therefore, to extend your consciousness in any direction you must secure evidence of the fact that there is more reality in that direction; and here we find the great mission of faith. Faith supplies this evidence. Faith looks further on into the beyond and sees real reality at every step, and proves to consciousness that things not seen are thoroughly substantial. Faith discerns that there is no danger in going on and on because there is solid ground all the way, no matter how far into the limitless we may wish to go; there is no danger of being lost in an empty void by following faith. Instead, faith gives us a positive assurance of finding more life, more power, more wisdom and a fairer state of existence than we ever knew before.

The practical value of faith is therefore to be found in its power to enlarge all the faculties and spheres of action in the mind of man, and as this enlargement can go on indefinitely, as there is no end to the visible, we conclude that anything can be accomplished by following faith. No matter how much wisdom or power we may require to reach the goal we have in view we can finally secure the required amount through the perpetual enlargement of consciousness. This is evident, and since faith is that something in mind that leads consciousness on and on into larger fields of action it becomes indispensable to all growth, to all great achievements, to all high attainments and to the realization of all true ideals. The man who has no faith in himself can neither improve himself nor his work. When nothing is added to his ability, capacity or skill there can be nothing added to the quality or the quantity of what he is doing. The effect will not improve until we have improved the cause; and man himself is the cause of everything that appears in his life.

Modern psychology, however, has discovered and conclusively demonstrated that no faculty can be improved until the conscious sphere of action of that faculty is enlarged and thoroughly developed. Therefore, to promote the efficiency of any faculty the conscious action of that faculty must become larger and imbued with more life. This is the fundamental principle in all advancement, but consciousness will not enlarge its sphere of action until it perceives that there is reality beyond its present sphere, and it is only through the interior insight of faith that the greater reality existing beyond present limitations is discovered to be real. The lack of this interior insight among the great majority is the principal obstacle that prevents them from becoming more than they are. Their minds have not the power to see the potential side of their larger nature. They are aware of the objective only and can do only as much as the limited power of the objective will permit. But they are not aware of the fact that there is limitless power within, nor do they realize that they can draw upon this great interior power and thus accomplish not only more and more, but everything that they may now have in view. Not having the power to look beyond present attainment, the little world in which they live is all that is real to them. Occasionally there is a dream or a vision of greatness, but it soon fades away, and in those rare instances when the high vision continues for some time the knowledge of how to make real the ideal is usually not at hand.

The human race is divided into three classes; first, those who live in the limited world and never see anything beyond the limited; second, those who live in the limited world but have occasional glimpses of greater things, though having neither the knowledge nor the power to make their dreams come true; and third, those who are constantly passing from the lesser to the greater, making real every ideal as soon as it comes within the world of their conscious comprehension. The last group is small, but there are millions today who are on the verge of a larger sphere of existence, and for this reason we should usher into the world at once a greater movement for the promotion of faith than has ever been known before. It is more faith that these millions need in order to enter into the beautiful life they can see before them. It is more faith they must have before they can become as much as they desire to be. It is faith, and faith alone, that can give them the power to do what this great sphere of existence may require.

To make real the ideal in any life faith must be combined with work, and no work should be undertaken unless it can be animated thoroughly with the power of faith. The reason why is found in the fact that all practical action is weak or strong, depending upon the capacity of that part of the mind which directly controls that action; and the capacity of the mind increases in proportion to the attainment of faith. To accomplish what we have in view, it is not only necessary to know how to go about our work, but it is necessary to have sufficient power, and faith is the open door to more and more power.

The very moment you obtain more faith you feel stronger; you are then certain of results and the very best results; and the reason why is found in the fact that faith always connects the mind with the larger, the greater and the inexhaustible. On the other hand, you may have an abundance of energy, but do not see clearly how to apply that energy in such a way that results will be as desired; again the remedy is more faith. Faith elevates the mind and lifts consciousness up above doubt, uncertainty and confusion. When you go up into faith you enter the light and can see clearly how to proceed; but in this connection we must avoid a very common mistake. When we discover the remarkable power of faith there is a tendency to depend upon faith exclusively and ignore other faculties. We sometimes come to the conclusion that it matters little how we work or think or act so long as we have an abundance of faith, because faith will cause everything to come right. The fact, however, that we sometimes come to this conclusion proves that we have not found real faith, because when we have an abundance of real faith we can see clearly the great truth that all thought and action must be right to secure results, and that all faculties and powers must be employed in their highest states of efficiency if we wish to make real the ideal. Though it is absolutely necessary to have the vision, still the vision is not sufficient in itself. After the vision has been discovered in the ideal it must be made real; the principle must be applied; the new discovery must be worked out in practical action; but these things require both fine intelligence and practical skill.

Faith without works is dead, because it does nothing, uses nothing, creates nothing; it is as if it were not; and works without faith are so insignificant and ordinary that they are usually very little better than nothing. But when work and faith are combined then everything becomes possible. The power of faith is placed in action; work becomes greater and greater, and whatever our purpose may be we shall positively scale the heights. The great principle is to combine unlimited faith with skillful work. Work with all the skill that you can possibly cultivate, but inspire all your efforts with the mighty soul of a limitless faith. Become as learned, as intellectual and as highly developed in mind as possible, but animate your prodigious intellect with the supreme spirit of faith. Faith does not come to take the place of art, skill or intellect. Faith comes to give real soul to art, skill and intellect. Faith comes to fill all physical and mental action with renewed life and power. It comes to open that door through which all our efforts may pass to higher and greater things. Faith is not simply for the moral and spiritual life; is not simply for what is sometimes called higher endeavor. It is for all endeavor, and it has the power to push all endeavor with such energy and force that we simply must succeed, no matter what our work may be. The man who has faith in his work, faith in himself, faith in the human race and faith in the Supreme, that man simply cannot fail, if he gives the full power of his faith to everything that he undertakes to do.

We must eliminate the idea that faith is something apart from everyday life, and that it is something for the future salvation of the soul only. We have held to that belief so long that real faith has actually been separated from human existence, and we find very few people today who really know what faith actually is. The fact is that if you are not giving your faith to everything you do, be it physical, mental or spiritual, you have not as yet obtained any faith. When faith comes it never comes to give greater power to a part of your life. It comes to give supreme power to all your life, and it comes to push all your work towards higher efficiency and greater results. When you have real faith you never undertake anything without first placing your entire being in the very highest attitude of faith. Even the most trivial things you do are done invariably in the spirit of faith. This is very important, because by training yourself to be at your best in little things it soon becomes second nature for you to be your best in all things, and when you are called upon to do something of exceptional importance, something that may seem very difficult, you do not fall down; you are fully equal to the occasion. The more we exercise faith the more it develops; it is therefore profitable to use faith at all times and in everything that we do.

When we know that faith is that something that takes mind into the superior side of life and thus places in action superior powers it is not difficult to understand how to proceed when we place ourselves in faith. As we think more and more of this higher side of our nature, this better side, this wonderful side, we gradually become conscious of its remarkable possibilities and soon we can feel the power of superiority becoming stronger and stronger in everything that we do in mind or body. To develop the power of faith the first thing to do is to train the mind to hold attention constantly upon the limitless side of life; that is, to live in the upper story of being and to think as much as possible about the true idea of faith, as well as the interior essence of faith itself. When you begin to see clearly that faith is this higher development of mind, this insight that leads to higher wisdom, greater power and more abundant life, you actually find yourself entering into the realization of those greater things whenever you think of faith. By concentrating your attention upon the inner meaning of faith your mind becomes clearer, your faculties become stronger and your entire being feels the presence of more life; and that you can do much better work while in this condition is too evident to require any more elucidation. While in the attitude of faith you cannot only do your present work better, but you will steadily develop the ability and the capacity to do more difficult work, work that will prove more useful to the community and more remunerative to yourself. The world wants everything well done and is more than willing to pay for good work. We are all seeking the best and the majority aim consciously or unconsciously to give their best, but without faith it is not possible for anyone to be his best, give his best, or do his best.

Do your best and the best will come to you in return. The universe is founded upon justice, and justice will positively be done to you if you have faith in justice. Everything in life is moving towards greater worth, and since justice is universal, the greater the worth of a man the greater the value of those things that he will receive in life. The worthy soul is always rich in those things that have real worth; and when we learn to harmonize ourselves more fully with all the laws of existence we shall place ourselves in that condition where we not only can give more that has worth but will also receive everything of worth that actually is our own. Whether you are working in the commercial world, the professional world, the artistic world, the intellectual world; in brief, whatever your work may be, to have the best results you must have faith, and it is practical results in practical everyday life that determines how rapidly and how perfectly the ideal shall be made real in your own world. Whoever will do his present work as well as he possibly can, and continue to work in the highest attitude of faith will positively advance and perpetually continue to advance. He may not have accomplished much thus far; but if he takes this course, combining efficient work with supreme faith, he certainly has a splendid future before him.

If your present work is not to your liking do not plan to change at once. First proceed with your present work in this higher attitude of faith. You may thus find your present work to be the very work you want; or your present work, if it is not what is intended for you, will become the open door through which you will reach that field of action that will be to your liking, providing you animate your present work with all the faith that you can possibly realize. Make yourself the best of your kind whatever your sphere of action may be, because by so doing you are not only increasing the number of great minds in the world, but you are adding immeasurably to the world's welfare and joy; and he who combines his work with limitless faith will become the greatest and the best in his sphere. In the application of faith, however, the whole of attention must not be directed upon the improvement of your work, but more especially upon the improvement of yourself. The more you improve the better work you can do, but while you are improving yourself your improvement will be incomplete and insufficient unless you each day practically employ in your work what you have developed in yourself. Give the power of every moment to greater attainment in yourself and to greater achievement in your present occupation, and you will fulfill that dual purpose in life that invariably leads to the heights. Develop more power, more ability and more faith and combine these in everything that you do. Through the power of faith you will not only discern higher and higher ideals, but you will also give greater capacity to your practical ability. In other words, you will not only gain the power to see the ideal, but you will gain the power to practically apply what you have seen; you will make tangible in real life what the visions of the soul have revealed in the ideal life; and as you grow in faith, so great will this power become that there is no ideal you cannot make real. You will have placed yourself in touch with limitless power, the power of the Supreme, and therefore to you, all things will become possible.

The Art Of Getting What is Wanted

We frequently hear the statement "I never received what I wanted until the time came when I did not care for it and did not need it." This statement may in most instances be based upon an unguided imagination, though this is not always the case, because there are thousands of people who actually have this very experience. They never get what they want until the desire for it, as well as the need of it, have disappeared. There may be occasional exceptions, but the rule is that what we persistently desire we shall sooner or later receive. Too often it is later, the reason being that most desires are purely personal and are not inspired by those real needs that may exist in the great eternal now. Mere personal desires are usually out of harmony with the present process of soul-growth, and therefore there is no supply in our immediate mental vicinity for what those desires naturally need. This is the reason why more time is required for the fulfilling of these desires, and frequently the time required is so long that when the desire is fulfilled we do not need it any more. When we desire only those things that are best for us now, that is, those things that are necessary to a full and complete life in the present, we shall receive what we desire at the very time when those things are needed. What is best for us now is ready in the mental world to be expressed through us. Every demand has its own supply in the immediate vicinity, and every demand will find or attract its own supply without any delay whatever, but the demand must be natural, not artificial.

The average person is full of artificial desires, desires that have been suggested by what other people possess or require. But the question is not what we need now to compete with other people so as to make more extravagant external appearances than other people. The question is, what do we need now to make our present life as full, as complete and as perfect as it possibly can be made now. Ask yourself this question and your artificial desires will disappear. In the first place, you will try to ascertain what you are living for, and what may be required to promote that purpose of life that may seem true to your deeper thought on the subject. In the second place, you will realize that since it is the present and the present only for which you are living you will concentrate your attention upon the living of life now. This will bring the whole power of desire down upon the present moment and engage all the forces of life to work for the perfection of the present moment. The result will be the elimination of nearly everything that is foreign to your present state of existence.

To know what to desire and what to ignore in the present may seem to be a problem, but it is easily solved by depending upon the demands of the soul instead of the demands of the person. The desires of the average person are almost constantly colored or modified by suggestions from the artificial life of the world; they are therefore not normal and are not true to real life. The desires of the soul, however, are always true and are always in harmony with the greatest good and the highest welfare of the entire being of man in his present sphere. It is the soul that lives; therefore the soul can feel truly what is necessary to fullness and completeness in present life. Real life never lives for the past or for the future. Real life lives now, and therefore knows the needs of life now. It is the soul that grows and develops; therefore the soul can feel what is required to promote present development. For these reasons it is perfectly safe to follow the desires of the soul and those desires only; it will mean the best of everything for body, mind and spirit, and the right things will appear in the right places at the right time.

We live not to acquire things nor to provide for an extravagant personal appearance. We live to become more than we are. We live to live a larger and a greater life perpetually; therefore every desire must desire only those things that are conducive to growth, advancement, attainment and superior states of existence. The expression of desire, however, must not confound cause with effect, but must so place every desire that the power of cause invariably precedes the appearance of effect. To promote advancement in life we must advance in our own conscious beings before true advancement in the external world can follow. Forced advancement is artificial, and is detrimental to the permanent welfare of the soul. Do not push the person forward. Live to give greater expression to the soul and you will develop all the power that is necessary to push the person forward towards any lofty goal you may have in view. Become more than you are from the within, and external environments, demands and opportunities will ask you to come forward. Thus you promote true advancement.

There are a number of people who believe that to follow the desires of the soul is to be led into poverty, and hardships in general, but those who have this belief know practically nothing about the real nature of the soul. He who follows the desires of the soul will be led away from sickness, trouble and poverty and will enter into the possession of the best of everything, physical, mental and spiritual. This is natural, because the ruling desire of the soul is to promote the attainment of greater power, greater ability, a larger life, superior qualities and greater capacity so that things may be done that are really worth while. The soul lives to unfold the limitless possibilities that are latent in the within. Therefore, to live the life of the soul and follow the desires of the soul is to become greater, more able, more competent and more worthy every day. By developing greater power in yourself you overcome sickness and trouble; and by constantly increasing your ability, your talent and your genius you pass from poverty to abundance, no matter where you may live or what your work may be.

The man who lives to perfect his entire being will naturally desire only those things that are conducive to the growth and the development that he is trying to promote, and such desires will be supplied without delay, because they are natural, and they are in harmony with real life. What life may require now that life can receive now. This is the law. But every artificial desire that we may hold in mind interferes with the workings of this law, and since the average person is full of artificial desires he usually fails to receive what is needed to promote the welfare of real life. Every desire that is held in mind uses up energy; therefore, if the desire is artificial, all that energy is thrown away, or it may be employed in creating something that we have no use for when it does come. It has been very wisely stated that a strong mind should weigh matters with the greatest of care before uttering a single prayer, because most of the prayers of such a mind are answered; and should he pray for something that he cares nothing for when it does come be will have a burden instead of a blessing.

The majority are entirely too reckless about their desires; they desire things because they want them at the time, but do not stop to think whether the things desired will prove satisfactory or not when they are received; and since we usually get, sooner or later, what we persistently desire, the art of knowing what to desire is an art, the development of which becomes extremely important. It is not an act of wisdom to pray for future blessings or to entertain desires that will not be fulfilled until some future time. When the future comes you may have advanced so far, or changed so much, that the needs of your life will be entirely different from what they are in the present. Let every desire be just for today, and let that desire be prompted by the ruling desire of your life; that is, the desire to become a more powerful personality, a stronger character, a more brilliant mind and a greater soul. Live perpetually in the desire that you will receive the best that life can give today, that all things will work together for good to you now, and that everything necessary to the promotion of your highest welfare will come in abundance during the great eternal now. Make this desire so strong that your heart and soul are in it with all the power of life, and let every present moment be deeply inspired by the very spirit of this desire. The result will be that the best of everything will constantly be coming into your world, and everything that may be necessary to make your life full and complete now will be added in an ever increasing abundance.

In this connection we must remember that is not best for anyone to pass through sickness, trouble and misfortune. When people have misfortune they sometimes console themselves with the belief that it is all for the best, but this is not the truth; though we can and should turn every adverse circumstance to good account. When you come into trouble you have not been living for the best. You have made mistakes or entertained artificial desires, and that is why trouble came. Had you lived in the faith that all things are working together for good, nothing but good would have come; and had you lived in the strong desire for the best and the best only, you would have received the very best that you could appreciate and enjoy now. The belief that we have to pass through trouble to reach peace and comfort is an illusion that we have inherited from the dark ages, and the belief that we are purified through the fires of adversity is another illusion coming from the same source. We are purified by passing through a perpetual refining process, and this process is the result of consciousness gaining a deeper, a higher, a truer and a more beautiful conception of that divinity in man that is created in the image and likeness of the Supreme; and it is well to remember that this refining process can live and act only where there is peace of mind, harmony of life and the joy of the spirit.

Higher states of life do not come by passing through adversity but by living the soul-life so completely that you are never affected by adversity. The peace that passeth understanding does not come from the act of overcoming trouble, but is the product of that state of mind that is so high and so strong that it is never moved by trouble. The greatest victory does not come through successful warfare, but through a life that is so high and in such perfect harmony with all things that it wars against nothing, resists nothing, antagonizes nothing, pursues nothing, overcomes nothing. The life that is above things does not have to overcome things, and it is such a life that brings real peace, true joy and sublime harmony. The belief that we have to fight for our rights is another illusion; likewise, the belief that wrongs have to be overcome. The higher law declares, be right in all things and you will have your rights in all things. Be above all things and you will not have to overcome anything. Live in the spirit of the limitless supply and you will not have to demand anything from any source, because you will be in the life of abundance.

There is value in the silent demand, but it is not the highest thought. The highest thought is to desire with heart and soul whatever we may need now, and live in the absolute conviction that all natural demands are supplied now; then we shall not have to make any demands whatever, silent or audible. A mental demand usually becomes a forced mental process, and such a process, though it may succeed temporarily, as all forced actions do, will finally fail; and when it does fail the mind will not be as high in the scale as it was before. The highest state is pure realization, a state where we realize that everything is at hand for us now and will be expressed the very moment we desire its tangible possession. Here we must remember never to turn our desires into mental demands, but to make every desire an inward soul feeling united perfectly with faith. The highest desire is always transformed into a whole-souled gratitude, even before the desire has been outwardly fulfilled, because when the desire is high in the spirit of faith it knows at once the prayer will be answered, and consequently gives thanks from the very depths of the heart.

The prayer that is uttered through the spirit of faith and through the soul of thanksgiving, the two united in one, is always answered, whether it be uttered silently or audibly. The desires that are felt in such a prayer are inspired by the divinity that dwells within and are therefore true to real life. They are soul desires. They belong to the present and will be fulfilled in the present at the very time when we want them and need them. When we fail to get what is wanted, our wants are either artificial or so full of false and perverted wants that the law of supply is prevented from doing its proper work for us. Under such conditions it is necessary to ask the great question, "What am I living for!" Then eliminate those desires that are suggested by the world, and retain only those that desire the highest state of perfection for the whole man. It is the truth that when man seeks first the kingdom of the true life, the perfect life, all other things needful to such a life will be added. He who desires more life will receive more life, and with the greater life comes the greater power, that power with which man may create his own destiny and make everything in his life as he wishes it to be. In order to get what is wanted or what is needed the usual process of desire must be reversed. Instead of desiring things, desire that greater life and that greater power that can produce things. First, desire life, power, ability, greatness, superiority, high personal worth, and exceptional spiritual attainments. Never desire definite environments, special things or certain fixed conditions. Leave those things to Higher Power, because when Higher Power begins to act you will receive the very best environments, the richest things and the most perfect conditions that you can possibly enjoy. Desire real life first, and all that is beautiful and perfect in the living of such a life in body, mind and soul, will invariably be added. Follow the desires of the soul and you will receive everything that is necessary, not only for the life of the soul but for the life of mind and body as well. Seek the Source of all good things and you will receive all good things.

Paths to Happiness

To be happy is the privilege of everybody, and everybody may be happy at all times and under all circumstances through the knowing and living of a few simple principles. The reason why happiness is not as universal and as abundant as it might be is because the majority seek happiness for itself alone. Happiness is an effect. It comes from a definite cause. Therefore, if we would obtain happiness we must not seek happiness for itself, but seek that something that produces happiness. He who seeks happiness directly, who desires happiness for the sake of gaining happiness or who works directly for the attainment of happiness will find but little real joy in his life. To seek happiness is to fail to find it, but to seek the cause of happiness is to find it in an ever increasing measure. Happiness, however, is not the result of any one single cause. It is the result of many ideal states of being grouped together into one harmonious whole. In brief, happiness is the result of true being perfectly lived upon all planes of consciousness. Happiness does not come from having much, but from being much; therefore, anything that will tend to bring forth into tangible expression more and more of the real being of man will add to his joy. To promote the larger and larger expression of the real being of man; in other words, to promote the living in the real of more and more of the ideal, a number of methods may be presented; but as happiness is based upon simplicity, methods for producing the cause of happiness must also be based upon simplicity, therefore only those principles that are purely fundamental need be employed. These principles however must not be applied singly. It is necessary to combine them all in practical everyday living, and when this is done, more and more happiness will invariably follow. The principles necessary to the perpetual increase of happiness are as follows:

1. Live the simple life. The complex life is not only a burden to existence, but is invariably an obstacle to the highest attainments and welfare of man; and the majority, even among those whose tangible possessions are very insignificant, are living a complex life; but when the average person is told to remove complexity from his world and adopt simplicity he almost invariably destroys the beauty of life. The art of living a life that is both simple and beautiful is an art that few have mastered, though it is by no means difficult. Most of the life that is called simple is positively devoid of beauty and has nothing whatever that is attractive about it. In fact, it is positively a detriment both to happiness and advancement. To live the simple life is not to return to primitive conditions nor to decide to be satisfied with nothing, or next to nothing. It is possible to live the simple life in the midst of all the luxuries that wealth can buy, because simplicity does not spring from the quantity of possession but from the arrangement of possession. The central idea in the living of a simple life is to eliminate non-essentials. The question should be, "Which of the things that are about me do I need to promote the greatest welfare of my life?" To answer this question will not be difficult, because almost anyone can determine at first thought what is needed and what is not needed to a complete life. When the decision is made, non-essentials should be removed as quickly as possible. True, we must avoid extremes, and whatever we do we must do nothing to decrease the beauty or the harmony of life.

There are a great many things in the world of the average person that he simply thinks he needs, though he knows that those things never did anything but retard his progress. It therefore necessary to remove non-essentials from the mind before we attempt to simplify our immediate surroundings. The simple life is a beautiful life, with all burdens removed, and it is only the unnecessary that is burdensome. To live the simple life, surround yourself only with those things that are directly conducive to your welfare, but do not consider it necessary to limit the quantity of those things. Surround yourself with everything that is necessary to promote your welfare, no matter how much it may be, although do not place in your world a single thing that is not a direct power for good in your world. You thus establish the harmony of simplicity without placing any limitations whatever upon your possessions, your welfare or your highest need. You thus eliminate everything that may act as a burden; and we can readily understand that when all burdens are removed from life the happiness of life will be increased to a very great degree.

2. Live the serene life. Be calm, peaceful, quiet and undisturbed in all things and at all times. Confusion and hurry waste energy, and it is a well known fact that depression and gloom are produced, in most instances, simply by the energy of the system running low. The serene life, if lived in poise, will keep the system brimful of energy at all tunes, and so long as you are filled through and through with life and energy you wilt be full of spirit and joy. Our saddest moments are usually the direct results of reactions from turbulent thinking and living; therefore, such moments will be eliminated completely when thinking and living are made peaceful and serene. It is not necessary to live the strenuous life in order to accomplish a great deal, although on the other hand it is not quantity but quality that we seek. Our object should not be to do many things, but to do good things. If we can do many things that are good, very well, but we must have duality first in the mind; the quantity will increase as we grow in capacity, and there is nothing that promotes the increase of mental and physical capacity more than calm, serene living. The sweetest joys that the mind can feel usually come from those deep peaceful realizations of the soul when all is quiet and serene. Therefore, to cultivate the habit of living always in this beautiful calm will invariably add happiness to happiness every day of continued existence.

3. Be in love with the world. He who loves much will be loved much in return, and there is nothing in the world that can give more joy and higher joy than an abundance of real love. The selfish love, that is only personal, and that must be gratified to be enjoyed, gives but a passing pleasure, the reaction of which is always pain. When we love with such a love we are always unhappy when not directly loved in return, and the purely selfish love never brings real love in return. When we love everybody with the pure love of the soul, that love that does not ask to be loved in return but loves because it is loved, we shall positively be loved in return; and not simply by a few here and there, but by great numbers. To feel that you are loved unselfishly, that you are loved not because anything is expected in return, but because the love is there and must come to feel this love is a source of joy which cannot be measured, and this joy everybody can receive in abundance now. The simple secret is to love the whole world at all times and under every circumstance; love everybody with heart and soul and mean it, and everything that hap-

pens to you will add both to the pleasure of the mind and to the more lofty joys of the soul.

4. Be useful. "Give to the world the best that you have and the best will come to you." Hold nothing back. If you have something that you can share with the world, let everybody have it today. Do all that you can for everybody, not because you expect reward, but because it is a part of your nature. Be all that you can be and do all that you can do. Never say, "I will do only as much as I am paid for." Such an attitude has kept many a person in poverty for life. Reward is an effect, not a cause. Do not place the reward first, and the service second. Increase your service and the reward will increase in proportion; you will thus not only place yourself in a position where you can secure more and more of the good things of life, but you will live in that position where you are bringing into expression more and more of the good things that exist in your own life. And we must remember that the greatest joy does not come from gaining good things from the without, but from the expression of good things from the within; and when both of these are combined harmoniously we shall secure all the joys of life, the joys that come from the outer world and the joys that come from the beauty and the splendor of the inner world. To combine these in your life, be useful; express your best; be your best; do your best. You thus bring forth riches from within and attract riches from without. Give richly of the best you have and good things in an ever increasing number will constantly flow into your life. That deep soul-satisfaction that comes to mind when we have rendered valuable service to man is entirely too good to be ignored; it is one of the deepest and highest joys that man can know. Those people who are the most valuable wherever they go are always the happiest, and we all can be of service in a thousand ways; therefore, we may add to our happiness in just as many ways, if we will always remember to be and do the best we can wherever we may go in the world.

5. Think and speak the beautiful only. Every word or thought that you express will return to you. Never say anything to make others discouraged or unhappy; it will come back to yourself. He who gives unhappiness to others is giving unhappiness to himself. He who adds to the joys of others is perpetually adding to his own joy. You can say something good about everybody. Then say it. It will give joy to everybody concerned, yourself included. Think only of the beautiful side of everybody. Everybody has a beautiful side. Find it and think of that only. You will thus live in the world of the beautiful, and he who lives in the world of the beautiful is always happy. Speak kindly and pleasantly

to everybody; think kindly and pleasantly of everybody, and your days of gloom will be gone. When every word is animated with the spirit of kindness and joy, you will not only increase the power of joy in your own life, but you will be sowing the seeds of joy in the garden of the universal life; and one of these days you will reap abundantly from what you have sown. Let this sowing time be continuous and the harvest will be continuous; thus you will be reaping a harvest of boundless joy every day of your endless existence.

6. Forgive and forget everything that seems wrong. We have spent many a weary day simply because we persisted in remembering something that was unpleasant. Forget the wrong and it will disturb you no more. Forgive others for what they have done and you will have no unpleasant memories to cloud the sky of your mental world. When people speak unkindly of you, never mind. Let them say what they, like, if they must. Nothing can harm you but your own wrong thinking and living. If people do not treat you right remember they would act differently if they knew better, and you know better than to become offended. So therefore forgive it all and resolve to be happy. Forgive everybody for what is not right and forget everything that is not conducive to the right. You have no time to brood over ills and troubles that exist only in your memory. Your memory is created for a better purpose. Remember the good, the true and the beautiful; this is one of the greatest secrets of perpetual happiness. When you forgive those who have wronged you, you usually come to a place where you think more of those very persons than you ever did before, and when you come to that place you will realize a joy that is far too sweet and beautiful for pen to ever describe. It seems to be a blessing coming direct from heaven and it does not go away. This fact proves that he who learns to forgive rises in the scale of life. He who can forget and forgive the wrongs of the lowlands of undeveloped life, invariably ascends to the heights, and it is upon the heights that we find real happiness. Such is the reward of forgiveness. It will therefore not be difficult to forgive when we know that the results are so rich and so beautiful; indeed, to forgive and forget everything that seems wrong will thus become a coveted pleasure.

7. Be perfectly contented with the present. We have heard a great deal about the value of divine discontent, but discontent is never divine any more than indignation is ever righteous. Perfect contentment is one of the highest states of the soul and is one of those attainments that invariably follows ideal living. Discontent, however, in any of its shapes or forms, always indicates that we are not on the true path. So long as

there is discontent there is something wrong in our living, but the moment this wrong is righted perpetual contentment will be realized. If your present lot is not what you wish it to be, discontent will not make it better. Be perfectly content with the present and create more lofty mansions for the future; thus you will not only improve your condition every year, but you will be supremely happy every day. The more perfect your present contentment the more power you will have to create for yourself a greater future, and the more mental light you will have to build wisely for days to come. The more contentment you realize in your mind the more brightness and strength there will be in your mind.

Find the good that you already possess, then enjoy it. Better things are even now on the way and through the harmony of contentment you will be prepared to receive them. You will also be in that higher state of mental discernment where you can know good things when you see them. Many people are so much disturbed by the discord of discontent that they are unable to recognize the good things already in their world; thus they add doubly to the cause of discontent. Contentment, however, does not mean to be so satisfied with present conditions that we do not care to change them. True contentment not only appreciates the full value of the present, but also appreciates those greater powers in life that can perpetually add to the value of the present; therefore, the contented mind gains everything that life can give in the great eternal now, while at the same time perpetually increasing the richness, the worth and the beauty of the great eternal now. To be contented, find fault with nothing. Those things that are not quite right can be made better. Proceed to make them better, and one of the greatest joys of life comes directly from that action of life that is causing things to become better. The process of growth and advancement is invariably conducive to joy; therefore, if we cease finding fault, and use all our time in promoting improvement, we will find sources of happiness in every imperfection that we may meet in life. In other words, when we aim to improve everything that we meet, we bring out all the good that is latent in our world, and to increase the expression of the good in our world is to increase our own measure of joy.

8. Seek the ideal. Look for the ideal everywhere; live in ideal environments when possible; but if not possible in an external sense create for yourself an ideal environment in the internal sense. Live in ideal mental worlds no matter what external worlds may be. Associate as much as possible with ideal people, and if you are living an ideal life in your own mental and spiritual life, you will attract ideal people wher-

ever you go. And one of the greatest joys of life is to associate with those who are living in lofty realms. We have no time to give to the common and the ordinary. We want the best. We deserve the best, and we can secure the best by seeking the best and the best only. Live your own ideal life. Seek the ideal both in the within and in the without, and aim to make the ideal real in every thought, word and deed; you will thus cause every moment to add to your joy.

9. Develop the whole man. To promote an orderly growth throughout your entire being is highly important, and to establish perfect harmony of action among all the various members of mind and body is indispensable to happiness. Develop everything in your nature and place all the elements in your being in perfect harmony. You will thus ascend perpetually to higher states of being and greater realms of joy. Much of the discord and unhappiness that comes into life is the direct result of one-sidedness and undevelopment, and these can be permanently removed only through the orderly development of the whole man. Body, mind and soul must be perfectly balanced in every sense of that term. The more perfectly you are balanced the greater will be your joy, because a balanced nature is conducive to harmony, and harmony is conducive to happiness.

10. Open the mind to beautiful thoughts only. The world is full of thoughts, all kinds of thoughts, but only those that are invited will come to you. There is nothing that affects life more than the thoughts we think; and the thoughts we are to think will depend almost entirely upon our mental attitude towards that which we meet in life. When we resolve to receive only beautiful thoughts from everything with which we come in contact the change for the better in life will be simply remarkable. All things will become new. We will actually enter a new heaven and a new earth, and the joys of existence will multiply many times.

11. Be in touch with the harmony of life. The universe is full of music, and happy is the soul that can hear the symphonies of heaven; he can find no greater joy. Every soul that has been in tune with higher things is familiar with that deep pleasure that comes to mind when the sensations of sublime harmony sweetly thrill every fibre of being; and we can all so live that we can be in tune with the music of the spheres. When you learn how to place yourself in harmony with the music of life you may for hours at a time remain within the gates of everlasting joy, and you may enter into the very life of that sublime something which eye has not seen nor ear heard. It is then that you understand why the

kingdom of heaven is within and why all souls that have found that inner life is radiant with joy. Here is happiness without measure, happiness that you may enjoy anywhere and at any time. No matter what your ,environments may be, enter into these lofty realms and you will be the happiest soul in the world.

12. Consecrate every moment to the higher life. The mind that is ever ascending can never be sad. Perpetual ascension means perpetual joy. The happiest moments that come to you are those moments that come when you see yourself rising in the scale of sublime existence. You are then ascending to the heights. You are entering into the cosmic realms, those realms where joy is supreme; and one single moment in that lofty realm gives more happiness than we can imagine were a million heavens united in one. It is in these realms that we enter the secret places of the Most High, and to enter into that sublime state is to gain all the happiness that life can give and have that happiness while eternity shall continue to be.

Creating Ideal Surroundings

We all believed, not so very long ago, that the circumstances in which each individual was placed were produced by inevitable fate, and that the individual himself could not change them, but would have to remain where he was until something in his favor happened from external sources. What was to cause that something to happen we did not know, nor did we give the matter much thought. We believed more or less in chance and luck, and had no definite conception of the underlying laws of things. But now many of us have changed our minds, as we have received a great deal of new light on this most important subject. The many, however, are still in the old belief; they are ignorant of the fact that man can create his own destiny, and that fate, circumstances and environments are but the products of man himself, acting alone, or in association with others. But this is the fact, and it can be scientifically demonstrated by anyone under any circumstance.

This new idea that man can change his surroundings or transport himself to more agreeable environments through the use of psychological and metaphysical laws may seem unthinkable and far fetched to a great degree; but when we study the subject with care we find that the principles, laws and methods involved are not only natural but thoroughly substantial and can be applied in tangible everyday affairs. If the surroundings in which you live are not what you wish them to be, know that you can change them. You can make those surroundings ideal. You can make those surroundings better and better at every step in your advancement, thus making real higher and higher ideals in your life.

This is a positive truth and should be impressed so deeply upon every mind that no former belief on the subject can cause us to doubt our possession of this power for a moment. The importance of thus impressing this fact upon the mind becomes very evident when we understand that no matter how much we may know, we will have no results so long as we are in doubt as to whether what we have undertaken is really possible or not. There are thousands of people who believe, in a measure, that they can better their own conditions and they understand fully all the principles involved, but they have no satisfactory results because one moment they believe that the change is possible while at the next moment they entertain doubts. To have real results in any undertaking, especially in the changing of one's surroundings, one must believe with his whole heart that he can, and he must constantly employ all the necessary principles in that conviction. No undertaking ever succeeded that was not animated through and through with the positive faith that it could be done, and such a faith is simply indispensable if you wish to create ideal surroundings for yourself, because the process depends directly upon the way you think. You must think that you can so as to fully annihilate the belief that you cannot. Know that you can, and in that attitude continue to apply the necessary methods. Let nothing disturb your faith in the possibility of what you have undertaken to do in this respect, and you will positively succeed.

To create ideal surroundings, the first essential is to gain a clear understanding of what actually constitutes your surroundings. The world in which you live is a state of many elements, factors, forces and activities. The physical environment with all its various phases and conditions has been considered the most important, but this is not necessarily true, because the mental environment is just as much a part of the world in which you live as the physical. The term "world" is not confined simply to visible things; it also includes states of mind, mental tendencies, thoughts, desires, motives and all the different phases of consciousness. The place in which you live physically, the place in which you live mentally, the place in which you live morally and spiritually, these places combined constitute the world in which you live. All of these states and conditions are necessary parts of your surroundings, and it is your purpose to make these necessary parts as beautiful, as perfect and as ideal as possible.

The place where you work with your hands and with your brain is a part of your world, but the same is true of the place where you work in your dreams, in your aspirations and in your ideals. The circumstances and events of your life, physically and mentally; the opportunities that are constantly passing your way; the people you meet in your work; the people you think of in your thoughts; the people you associate with and friends that are near; the various elements of nature, both visible and invisible; the many groups of things in all their various phases that you come in contact with in your daily living; all of these belong in your world. To enter into details it would be possible to mention many hundreds of different elements or factors that compose the world in which the average person lives; but to be brief we can say that your world is composed of everything that enters your life, your home, your experience, your thought and your dreams of the ideal. All of these play their part in bringing to you the good that you may desire or the ills that you may receive. Consequently, since the world in which you live is so very complex and since so much of it belongs to the mental side of life, the process of change must necessarily involve mental laws, as well as physical laws; but here the majority have made their mistake.

Many great reformers and human benefactors have tried to emancipate the race through the change of exterior laws and external conditions alone, forgetting that most of the troubles of man and nearly all of his failures have their origin in the misuse of the mind. We all know that mind is the most prominent factor in the life of man, and yet this factor has been almost entirely overlooked in our former efforts to change the conditions of the race. Everything that man does begins in his mind; therefore, every change that is to take place in the life of man must begin in his mind. This being true, we understand readily why modern metaphysics and the new psychology can provide the long looked for essentials to human emancipation and advancement. When we examine all the various things that go to make up the world in which we live we may find it difficult to discover the real source of them all. How they were produced; who produced them; why they happened to come to us, or why we went to them; these are problems that we are called upon to solve before we can begin to create ideal surroundings.

To solve these problems the first great fact to realize is that we are the creators of our own environments; but at first sight this fact may not be readily accepted, because there are so many things that seem to be the creation of others. There are two kinds of creation, however, the direct and the indirect. In direct creation you create with the forces of your own life, your own thought and your own actions, and your own creations are patterned after the ideas in your own mind; but in what is termed indirect creation some one else creates what you desire. It is your creation, however, in a certain sense, because it was your desire that called it forth. To state the fact in another manner, the world in which you live may be your own direct creation or it may be the creation of another, but you went into that other one's world to live. In the majority of cases, the world in which the individual lives is produced partly by his own efforts and partly by the efforts of others, though there is nothing in his world that he has not desired or called forth in some manner and at some time during his existence. There are a number of people who are living in worlds created almost entirely by others; in fact, the world of the average person is three-fourths the creation of the race mind; but the question is, why does a person enter into a world that is created by others; why does he not live exclusively in a world created by himself?

There are many fine minds who are living in the world of the submerged tenth, but they did not create that world. That inferior state existed long before the birth of its present inhabitants; but why have those gone to live there who were not born there, and why have those who were born there not gone away to some better world of their own superior creation? Why do the people who live in that inferior world continue to perpetuate all its conditions? No world can continue to exist unless the people who live in that world continue to create those conditions that make up that world. Then why do not those people who live in the world of the submerged tenth cease the creating of that inferior world and begin the creation of the superior world when we know they have the power to do so? These are great questions, but they all have very simple answers. To answer these questions the first great fact to be realized is that the mind of man is the most important factor in everything that he does, and since no person can change his environments until he changes his actions we realize that the first step to be taken is the change of mind. Learn to change your mind for the better, and you will soon learn how to change your surroundings for the better. Before you proceed, however, there is another important condition to be considered; it is the fact that a portion of what is found in our world is created by ourselves, while the rest is the product of those minds with which we work or live. In the home each individual contributes to the qualities of the world which all the members of that home have in common, but each individual lives in a mental world distinctly his own, unless he is so negative that he has not a single individual purpose or thought. When the mental world of each individual is developed to a high degree it will become so strong that the fate of that individual will not be affected by the adverse conditions that may exist in the home.

The same is true of the environments that we meet in our places of work. No man need be affected very long by adverse surroundings or obstacles that he may meet in his work. He will finally become so strong that he can overcome every adversity that may exist in his physical world and thus gain entrance to better surroundings. However, we can readily see how a great deal of discord can be produced in a home or in our place of work where the different members are not in harmony with each other, and we can also understand how the events, circumstances and conditions of all those members, as well as each individual member, will be affected more or less by that in harmony; providing however, that each individual is not developing that power of his mental world that can finally overcome all adversity. We can also understand how harmony and cooperation in a home or in a place of work would become a powerful force for good in the life of each individual concerned. Where a few are gathered in the right attitude there immense power will be developed; in fact, sufficient power to do almost anything that those few may wish to have done. This has been fully demonstrated a number of times; therefore, where many minds are associated in the creation of a world in which all will live, more or less, these higher mental laws should be fully understood and most thoroughly applied.

To enter a world that does not correspond with yourself and to go in and live where you do not naturally belong is to go astray, and such an action will not only cause all the forces and elements of your life to be misdirected, but you will place yourself in that position where nothing that is your own can come to you. There are vast multitudes, however, who have gone astray in this manner, and that is the reason why we find so many people who are misplaced, who do not realize their ideals, and who have not the privilege to enjoy their own. But we may ask, why do people go astray in this manner; why do we associate with people that do not belong in our world; why do we enter environments that do not correspond to our nature; why do we enter vocations for which we are not adapted, and why do we pursue plans, ideas and ambitions that lead us directly away from the very thing that our state of development requires? These are questions that we must answer, because no one can get the greatest good out of life or make the most of himself unless he lives in a world where he truly belongs. It is only when you live in a world created by yourself or in a world that others have created in harmony with you that you can be your real self, and since one must be truly himself to be wholly free and to promote his own advancement naturally and completely the subject is of great importance.

There are two reasons why we stray from our own true world and enter worlds where we do not belong; first, because we frequently permit the inferior side of our nature to predominate; and second, because we permit the senses to guide us in almost everything that we do. No person who has qualifications for the living of life in a superior world will ever enter an inferior world if he does not permit inferior desires to lead him into destructive paths; and no person, no matter what his work may be, will go down the scale so long as he follows the highest mental and spiritual light that he can possibly see during his most lofty moments. Follow the highest and the best that is in you, and you will constantly ascend into higher and better worlds; all your creative forces will thus build for you better and better surroundings, because so long as you are rising in the scale everything in your life in the external as well as in the internal must necessarily improve continuously. There is no need whatever of any person ever entering an inferior world. No one need pass into environments and surroundings that are less desirable than the ones in which he is living now. In fact, a person may take the opposite course. Endeavor constantly to attain superiority and you will steadily work yourself up into superiority, and as you become superior you will find an entrance into those worlds, those environments and those surroundings that are superior. There is a higher light, a better understanding within yourself that will guide you correctly in all your associations with people and environments. Do not follow physical desires or physical senses; let these be servants in the hands of higher wisdom. Follow this higher wisdom and you will make few mistakes, if any. You will constantly pass into better and better surroundings, because you will constantly pass into a higher, a better and a superior life. To follow the highest and the best that is within you under all circumstances does not constitute supernaturalism. It is simply good sense enlarged, and those who take this course will continue to make real the ideal in everything that may exist in the world in which they live. In consequence, both the mental world and the physical world in which we live will perpetually change for the better; and all our surroundings will improve accordingly, becoming more and more ideal until everything that exists about us is as beautiful as the visions of the soul.

Changing Your Own Fate

When you discover that you are living in a world that you did not create and that does not correspond with your ideals, there is a tendency to break loose from external conditions at the earliest possible moment; but this tendency must be checked. Nothing is gained through an attempt to change from one world of effect to another world of effect without first changing the cause. The majority believe that, when things are wrong in the outer world the only remedy is to change external conditions; but the fact is that external conditions are simply effects from internal causes, and so long as those internal causes remain the same, no attempt to change external conditions will prove of permanent value. So long as there are adverse causes in your inner life there will be adverse effects in your outer life, no matter how many times you may change from one condition to another or from one place to another.

When you begin to seek emancipation from the false world in which you are living now; in other words, when you begin to take positive measures to change your own fate, the first thing to do is to resolve not to make any forceful effort to change external conditions without first changing the inner cause of those conditions. Let outer things be as they are for the time being and continue to remain where you are until you can open a door to better things; but while you are waiting for this door to open do not be idle in any manner whatever. Although you are letting things be as they are in the external sense, and although you are not forcing yourself into different places or circumstances, still your purpose must be to entirely remake yourself. You came into this false state of life because you were misled by your own judgment, and if you should break loose, this same judgment will mislead you again; you will thus pass from one world that is not your own into some other world that is not your own, and there will be no improvement in the change. If you have not improved yourself in any manner whatever, your judgment will be just as inferior and unreliable as it was before, and no attempt to follow this judgment into different conditions will help matters in the least. Your object is not to set yourself free from the false world in which you are living now and then enter some other world that is not your own. You are not ready to move, neither physically nor mentally, until you have created a world of your own just as you would have it in your present state of development. Therefore, all thought of change will but divert your attention from the real purpose in view. So long as you are constantly thinking about external changes your mind cannot concentrate upon internal changes. So long as you are trying to change external conditions you cannot change yourself, and as you, yourself, are the cause of the new world which you are trying to create, you must recreate yourself before you can create the external world as desired.

To change your fate begin with yourself. If the environments in which you live are beneath your ideal, nothing can be gained by leaving those environments until the way is opened naturally to better things. If you simply get up and leave, you will gravitate into something elsewhere that will be just as uncongenial as those conditions you left behind. First, find the reason why you are living in your present adverse environments, then proceed to remove that cause. There may be many reasons, but in most cases the principal reason is a lack of ability or the lack of power to apply the ability you possess. In such a case you must remove inability by becoming more proficient, and as soon as you are competent to render better service you will readily find a better place. This means larger remuneration, and you will thus be able to secure more desirable surroundings. The many, however, will think that to promote sufficient improvement so as to command greater recompense, and do so in a short time, is practically impossible under the average conditions; but all difficulties that may be met in this connection may be readily removed through the principles of modern metaphysics.

Continuous improvement in everything pertaining to the life, the power, the capacity or the mentality of the individual can be readily promoted by anyone and decided results secured in a very short time. Therefore, no person need remain in adverse or limited conditions. He can, through the awakening and the expression of the best that is in himself, become competent to take advantage of greater opportunities and thus change his fate, his future and his destiny. If you wish to improve your physical environments, remain content where you are while you develop the power to earn and create better environments. Contentment with things as they are and harmony with everything about you are indispensable essentials if you wish to increase your ability, your capacity and your worth. To continue to kick against the pricks is to remain where pricks are abundant; but when we cease this mode of action and begin to polish off all the rough corners of our nature and improve ourselves in every manner possible, things will take a turn. We will leave the world of pricks and enter a smoother path. The polished man is admitted to the polished world where there are no rough places and where adverse conditions are few, if existing at all. When circumstances are against you, do not contend with circumstances. So long as we contend with things, things will contend with us. Do not resist present conditions; you prolong their existence by so doing. Whatever comes, meet all things in the attitude of perfect harmony and you will find that all things, even the most adverse, can be readily handled and turned to good account. We all know the marvelous power of the man who can harmonize contending factions, be they in his own life or in his circumstances. He not only gains good from everything that he meets, but he becomes a most highly respected personage, and is sought wherever opportunities are great and where great things are to be accomplished. Learn to harmonize the contending factions in your own life and experience, and you will find yourself entering new worlds where circumstances are more congenial and opportunities far greater. You will thus meet more desirable events, more desirable people, and superior advantages of every description will appear in your pathway. If your present friends are not to your liking admire them nevertheless for every good quality that they may possess. Emphasize their good qualities and ignore everything in their nature that seems inferior. This will help you to develop superior qualities in yourself; and this is extremely important, because as you develop superiority you prepare yourself for places higher up in the scale.

Make yourself over, so to speak, in your own friendship; increase your personal worth; polish your own character; refine your mind, and make real more and more of the ideal; double and treble your love and your kindness and constantly increase your admiration for everything that has real quality and high worth. Continue thus until you have results, whether those results begin to come at once or not; they will positively come ere long, and the things that you develop in yourself you will meet in your external world. Change yourself for the better in every shape and manner, and you change your fate for the better, but the change that you produce in yourself must not simply be negative in its action. It is the positive character, the positive mind, the positive personality that meets in the external world what has been developed in the internal world. The fact that a change in yourself can produce a similar change in your fate, your environments, your circumstances, in brief, everything in your outer world, may not seem clear at first; but it is easily demonstrated to be the truth when we analyze the relationship that exists between man and the world in which he lives. Everything that exists in your outer world has a correspondent in your inner world. This inner correspondent is the cause that has either created or attracted its external counterpart, and the process is easily understood.

To state it briefly, environment corresponds with ability. Circumstances are the aggregation of events brought about by your own actions and associations and friends, which follow the law of like attracting like. That environment is the direct effect of ability may not seem true when we observe that there are many people living in luxury that have practically no ability, but we must first demonstrate that these people have no ability. We shall find that those who have actually accumulated their own wealth have ability, in fact, exceptional ability, though they may not always have employed it according to the exact principles of justice. On the other hand, when we understand the process of creation we shall find that ability employed according to principle will produce far greater results than when it is employed unjustly. Therefore, the law underlying the power of ability to create its own environment acts wholly in the favor of him who lives according to the highest ideals of life.

This fact becomes more evident when we discern that success is not measured simply by the accumulation of things, but also by the accumulation of those elements in life that pertain to quality and worth in man's interior nature. It is wealth in the mental and the spiritual worlds that has the greatest value or the greatest power in promoting the welfare and the happiness of man, and this higher wealth can be accumulated only by those who are living according to their ideals. However, the accumulation of mental and spiritual wealth will have a direct tendency to increase the power and the capacity of practical ability, and practical ability when scientifically applied will tend to increase tangible wealth; that is, to improve the value and the worth of external environments. When we consider this subject from the universal viewpoint we shall find a perfect correspondent existing between the size of a man's possessions, physical, mental and spiritual, and the size of his brains, taking the term "brains" to signify ability, capacity and worth in the largest sense; but the size of brains can be increased perpetually. We therefore conclude that possessions in the larger sense can be increased perpetually, and he who is perpetually increasing his possessions on all the planes of his life is constantly changing his fate for the better. We shall also find that when a person increases the power of his own life he will bring about, through his own actions, new events, and these new events will produce new circumstances.

To change circumstances is to change fate; and whatever the change may be in fate, circumstances or events it will be a change for the better, if the increase of power is applied according to the principles of ideals. Again, when a person develops quality and superiority in himself he will, through the law of attraction, meet friends and associations that are after his own heart. In other words, he will enter a world where his ideals, both as to persons and as to things, are constantly being made real in every sphere of his present state of existence. He is thus creating for himself a better fate in every sense of the term and opening doors and pathways to a larger and a more beautiful future than he has ever realized before; but the beginning is in himself; in fact, every change for the better must begin within the life of man himself, and whoever will begin to change for the better in the within will positively realize greater and greater changes for the better in the without.

Building Your Own Ideal World

To build your own ideal world, the first essential is to begin to build in the real everything that you can discern in the ideal; and the second essential is to continue to rebuild your ideal world according to higher and higher ideals. However congenial or desirable or perfect our world may be, we should continue to improve upon it constantly. When we cease to promote progression we return to the ways of retrogression. One of the principal causes of undesirable environments or unexpected reverses among the more capable is found in the tendency to "'stop, rest and enjoy" what we have gained whenever conditions are fairly satisfactory. It is the mind that is ever creating the new and ever recreating everything according to higher ideals that is always free and that is always enjoying the best. No one can be in bondage to the lesser who is constantly rising out of the lesser, and he who is ever growing into the best is constantly enjoying the best. In the last analysis, retrogression is the only cause of bondage, while constant progression is the only cause of perfect freedom; and constant progression is promoted by the continuous recreation of everything in your world according to higher and higher ideals.

To begin, your entire mentality must be changed and constantly changed so as to correspond perfectly with your newest thoughts on every subject and your highest ideals of everything that you can discern in your life. The mind is the cause and is the source of every force that can act as a cause of whatever may be developed, expressed or worked out through yourself into your external world. Therefore, begin with the mind and with all the elements of the mind. All desires, motives and ambitions must be concentrated upon the larger and the perfect in their various spheres of action. All the mental states must be in harmony with each other, and with the outer as well as the inner conditions of life. All mental qualities must be expanded and enlarged constantly, and consciousness must be trained to act perpetually upon the verge of the limitless. The entire world of thought must be perpetually renewed, enlarged and perfected, and every step taken in the mental world must be practically expressed and applied in the outer world. In order to bring all the creative forces of mind into harmony with the goal in view the ideal wished to be realized must be thoroughly established in consciousness, and the goal in view must be constantly held before the mental vision. In the rebuilding of your own world one of the principal causes of failure will be found in a tendency to change your plans, motives or desires; therefore, do not permit yourself to entertain one group of desires today and a different group tomorrow, and do not permit your faith to fall into periodical states of doubt. Decide upon what you wish to do, accomplish, promote and attain, and proceed to live, think and work for those things, regardless of what may happen. The powers within you follow the predominating states of mind, and when these states are constantly changing, the creative forces will be employed simply in taking initial steps, but never in completing anything. On the other hand, when your mental states, desires, motives, plans, etc., continue to concentrate upon the one supreme goal in view your creative forces will perpetually build towards that goal, and you will be daily rebuilding your entire world according to the higher, the better and the greater that you have in view. There are thousands of fine minds that are down in the scale today and cannot get up, because they are constantly changing their plans, motives and desires. To create a new world you must fix in your mind what you wish to create, and then continue to build until the complete structure is finished. Recreate your present world, then constantly make it better, larger and more beautiful. All the elements of your mind, both conscious and subconscious, must be constantly inspired with your highest thought of the larger, the better and the more beautiful. Not a single thought should enter your mind that is inferior or in the least beneath your ideal of life, and not a single moment of discouragement or doubt should ever be permitted. Fix your mind on the soul's vision and hold it there through all sorts of circumstances or conditions. Do not waver for a moment. Keep the eye single upon the heights and all the powers of your being will build that great world that you can see in your mental vision as you concentrate attention upon the heights.

The mind must be clean, strong and high. It is the mind that does things. It is the mind that originates things. Therefore, if you wish to build for yourself an ideal world, the mind must be ideal in every sense of the term, and every element of the mind must always be its best and act at its best. To promote the right use of mind the imagination must be guided with the greatest of care. The imagination is one of the most important powers in the mind. The imagination when misdirected can produce more ills than any other faculty, and when properly directed can produce greater good than any other faculty. In fact, the imagination when scientifically applied becomes a marvelous power in the great creative process of the vast mental domain. Train the imagination to picture, not only the goal you have in view but all the highest ideals that you can possibly imagine as might exist within the realms of that goal. Train the imaging faculty to impress upon the mind only those superior qualities that you wish to incorporate in your new world, and whatever you impress upon the mind will be created in your mental world. To create superior qualities in the mental world means that you will create, as well as attract, the superior in your outer world, and you thus promote the building of an ideal world.

To build your own ideal world, the more opportunities that you can take advantage of the better, but opportunities come only to those who have demonstrated their worth. Prove to the world that you have worth, and you can have your choice of almost any opportunity that the world can offer. There is nothing that is in greater demand than great men and women, minds of ability and power, people who can do things. The great mind is constantly in the presence of opportunities to change his environment and his field of action; therefore, he may enter into a new world almost any time. Those opportunities, however, do not come of themselves; they come because he has made himself equal to those opportunities. Make yourself equal to the best and you will meet the best. This is a law that is universal and is never known to fail. Make yourself a great power in your present sphere of action. Learn to do things better than they have ever been done before. Produce something for the world that the world wants and the gates to new and greater opportunities will open for you. Henceforth, you may secure almost anything that you may wish, and all the elements that may be necessary for you to employ in order to build the ideal world you have in mind may be readily obtained because you have placed yourself in touch with the limitless supply of the best that life can give.

Those who are in search for new and greater opportunities should eliminate the belief that the best things have been said, that all great things have been done and that all remarkable discoveries have been made. The fact is we are just in the A B C of literature, invention, art, music, industrial achievements and extraordinary human attainments. The human race is now on the verge of hundreds of undeveloped fields that have just been discovered, and they have more possibilities in store than we have ever dreamed. Many of these possibilities when developed will supply the world with the very things that the present development of the race is demanding in every expression of thought and desire. It is therefore easier to attain greatness, and do something of exceptional value at the present time than it ever was before. The opportunities of this age are very numerous, and some of them hold possibilities that are actually marvelous. Those who will prepare themselves to meet the requirements of this age will therefore find a number of rich fields already at hand, and all minds can prepare themselves as required. Every person of moderate intelligence can, in a short time, place himself in the path of some of these new opportunities, and all minds can find better opportunities in their present spheres if they will proceed to become more than they are.

Train all the elements of your being to work towards a higher goal and you will bring forth into expression those greater powers that will make for you a mentality that the world will demand for its highest places of action and achievement. When you proceed to build in yourself an ideal mental world, a mental world of power, ability, capacity and high worth you will find it necessary to adapt this mental world to the external world in such a way as to promote harmony of action. The added power of your new mental world must work in harmony with your external world if practical results are to be secured. Circumstances come from personal actions; therefore, to change circumstances, personal actions must be changed, and to change personal actions your ideal mental life must be expressed in your personal life, and to this end the development of a high degree of harmony becomes necessary. Harmony, however, will not only promote the united action of the inner world with the outer world, but will also tend to eliminate mistakes from personal actions, and when we eliminate, mistakes from personal actions we will cease to produce adverse circumstances. When you are in perfect harmony with yourself and everything you eliminate mental confusion. You thus place your mind in that position where you can think clearly, reason logically and judge wisely. The result is, you will do the right thing at the right time. The elements of your life will be properly blended, and this is necessary in order to create an ideal world.

Another essential in the practical application of your ideals to real life is the development of what may be termed interior insight. This faculty will guide you perfectly in your expression of the finer things of life through the tangible things of life; in other words, you will see clearly how to combine the ideal with those actions that are promoted for the purpose of rebuilding the real. To combine the ideal with the real and make the two one, we must come into the closest possible relationship with the finer things in life and learn to use that phase of mind that is always in a cleared-up condition. The lower story of the mind is often darkened with false conclusions about things, and is frequently more or less filled with ideas that have been impressed through the senses; but in the upper story we can see things, as they are; we can think clearly, and invariably come to the right conclusions. The power to think in the upper story of the mind, the cleared-up side of consciousness where the sun is always shining and where there are no clouds, is called interior-insight. This interior insight not only discerns the ideal, but can discern the practical possibilities that every ideal may contain, and we make the ideal real when we proceed to develop and apply in actual life those practical possibilities that our ideals may contain. Interior insight will also elevate all our mental faculties and cause those faculties to function with far greater efficiency. In fact, the entire mind will be lifted up into a state of greater power, greater brilliancy and greater ability for high and efficient mental expression.

To develop interior insight, aim to use consciousness in the discernment of what may be termed the spirit of all things. Do not simply think of things as they appear on the surface, but try to think of things as they are in the spirit of their interior existence. The mere effort to do this will develop the power to look through things or to look into things; and the growth of this power promotes interior insight. You may thus discern clearly the real worth and the real possibilities that exist in the lofty goal that you have in view, and by keeping the eye single upon that lofty goal, never wavering for a moment, all the powers of your being will work together and build for those greater things that you can see upon the heights of that goal. Thus your entire world in the within as well as in the without will constantly be recreated and rebuilt according to the likeness of your supreme ideals; in consequence, you will not only build for yourself an ideal world, but you will be building for yourself a world that is ever becoming more and more ideal, and to live in such a world is ideal living indeed. The world that is ever becoming more and more ideal is the world in which to live, and the power to create such a world is now at hand in every human mind.

www.ingramcontent.com/pod-product-compliance
Lightning Source LLC
LaVergne TN
LVHW090958080826
845145LV00003B/1049

* 9 7 8 1 6 0 4 5 0 0 0 6 6 *